SCRIPTURE UNION

KU-739-393

BIBLE CHARACTERS AND DOCTRINES

**Philip to
The Church in Jerusalem**
E. M. BLAIKLOCK, M.A., D.Litt.

The Holy Spirit
LEON MORRIS, M.Sc., M.Th., Ph.D.

SCRIPTURE UNION
5 WIGMORE STREET
LONDON, W1H OAD

© 1974 Scripture Union
First Published 1974

ISBN 0 85421 315 5

Printed and bound in England by
Cox & Wyman Ltd, London, Reading and Fakenham

INTRODUCTION

This series of S.U. Bible Study aids takes its place alongside our existing range of Notes and Bible Study Books.

Each volume of Bible Characters and Doctrines is divided into the right number of sections to make daily use possible, though dates are not attached to the sections because of the books' continuing use as a complete set of character studies and doctrinal expositions. The study for each day is clearly numbered and the Bible passage to be read is placed alongside it.

Sections presenting the characters and doctrines alternate throughout each book, providing balance and variety in the selected subjects. At the end of each section there is a selection of questions and themes for further study related to the material covered in the preceding readings.

Each volume will provide material for one quarter's use, with between 91 and 96 sections. Where it is suggested that two sections should be read together in order to fit the three-month period, they are marked with an asterisk.

The scheme will be completed in four years. Professor E. M. Blaiklock, who writes all the character studies, will work progressively through the Old and New Testament records. Writers of the doctrinal sections contribute to a pattern of studies drawn up by the Rev. Geoffrey Grogan, Principal of the Bible Training Institute, Glasgow, in his capacity as Co-ordinating Editor. A chart overleaf indicates how the doctrinal sections are planned.

In this series biblical quotations are normally taken from the RSV unless otherwise identified. Occasionally Professor Blaiklock provides his own translation of the biblical text.

DOCTRINAL STUDY SCHEME

	Year 1	Year 2	Year 3	Year 4
First Quarter	The God who Speaks	Man and Sin	The Work of Christ	The Kingdom and the Church
Second Quarter	God in His World	Law and Grace	Righteousness in Christ	The Mission of the Church
Third Quarter	The Character of God	The Life of Christ	Life in Christ	The Church's Ministry and Ordinances
Fourth Quarter	The Holy Trinity	The Person of Christ	The Holy Spirit	The Last Things

DOCTRINAL STUDIES
THE HOLY SPIRIT

Study

A Divine Person

1 Grieving the Holy
   Spirit   Isaiah 63.7–14; Ephesians
   4.25–32

2 The Spirit in the
   Church   Haggai 2.1–9; Acts 5.1–11
3 The Spirit Within   1 Corinthians 2
4 The Spirit Sets Men
   Free   Romans 8.9–11;
   2 Corinthians 3

5 The Temple of God   1 Corinthians 3.16, 17;
   2 Corinthians 6.14–7.1

6 Three Mighty Persons   Matthew 28.16–20;
   1 Corinthians 12.4–6;
   2 Corinthians 13.14

Active in the Universe

12 Creator Spirit   Genesis 1.1, 2; Psalm 33.6–9
13 The Breath of God   Genesis 2.4–7; Job 32.6–10;
    33.1–7

14 Life depends on God   Job 34.10–15; Psalm
    104.24–30

Employing Human Instruments under the Old Covenant

15 The Skill of the
    Craftsman   Exodus 28.1–4; 31.1–11;
    35.30–35

16 The Spirit and the
    Elders   Numbers 11.16, 17, 24–30
17 The Strength of Samson   Judges 13.24–14.20
18 The Spirit and the
    spirits   1 Samuel 16
19 Denouncing Evil   Micah 3.5–12

Study

Preparing for the Messiah's Advent

24 The Spirit of Wisdom   Isaiah 11.1–9
25 The Servant of the Lord   Isaiah 42.1–4; 61.1–4
26 The Transforming
    Spirit   Isaiah 32.9–20; 43.25–44.5
27 The Vindication of God   Ezekiel 36.22–38; 39.25–29
28 The Spirit and All
    Flesh   Joel 2.15–32
29 The Forerunner   Luke 1.13–17, 39–45
30 The Glory and the
    Gloom   Luke 2.22–35
31 John's Witness to the
    Spirit   John 1.19–34

The Spirit and the Lord Jesus

39 Holy Child, Son of God   Luke 1.26–38
40 Beginning with the
    Spirit   Luke 3.21, 22; 4.1–21
41 The Ultimate
    Blasphemy   Luke 11.9–13; 12.8–12
42 Anointed with the
    Holy Spirit   Acts 10.34–43

His Coming at Pentecost

54 The Paraclete   John 14.15–18, 25–27
55 Convincing the World   John 15.18–16.15
56 Jesus and the Spirit   John 7.37–39; 20.19–23
57 The Promise and the
    Power   Luke 24.44–53; Acts 1.1–14
58 The Coming of the
    Spirit   Acts 2.1–21, 36–42

The Spirit and the Growing Church

68 Filled with the Spirit   Acts 4
69 The Serving of Tables   Acts 6.1–10; 11.19–24
70 The Spirit and the
    Samaritans   Acts 8.1–24
71 The Spirit and the
    Gentiles   Acts 10.44–11.18

Study

72 The Spirit and the
      Missionaries   Acts 13.1–12
73 The Spirit and the
      Baptism of John   Acts 18.24–19.7

The Spirit and the Christian Life

77 The Spirit and the Law   Galatians 3.1–14
78 The Spirit and the
      Flesh   Galatians 5.13–6.10
79 The Law of the Spirit
      of Life   Romans 8.1–27
80 The Gifts of the Spirit 1 Corinthians 12
81 Love is the Greatest   1 Corinthians 13
82 Speaking in 'Tongues'   1 Corinthians 14
83 The Seal and the
      Pledge   2 Corinthians 1.21, 22;
                             5.1–5; Ephesians 1.11–14
84 The Spirit and Wisdom   Ephesians 1.15–23; 3.14–21
85 Exhilaration in the
      Spirit   Ephesians 5.15–21; 6.10–20
86 All have Knowledge   1 John 2.18–27; 3.23, 24

The Spirit and the Holy Scriptures

94 God has Spoken   2 Samuel 23.1–7;
                             Mark 12.35–37
95 'God-breathed'   2 Timothy 3.10–17
96 Scripture's Origin   2 Peter 1.16–2.3;
                             1 John 4.1–6
97 The Spirit and the
      Tabernacle   Hebrews 9.1–10; 10.11–18

CHARACTER STUDIES
PHILIP
TO
THE CHURCH IN JERUSALEM

Study

7	Philip	John 14
8	The Branches	John 15
9	The Ordained	John 16
10	The Sleepers	Matthew 26.36–46; Luke 22.39–46
11	The Youth in the Garden	Mark 1.1–8; 14.1–52
20	Annas	John 18.1–14; Psalm 22.1–13
21	Caiaphas	John 11.47–57; Exodus 23.1–8
22	The False Witnesses	Matthew 26.57–68; Deuteronomy 19.16–20
23	Peter	John 18.15–27
32	The Procurator	Luke 13.1–3; Acts 3.12–19
33	The Judge	John 18.28–40; Luke 23.1–7
34	Pilate and Truth	John 8.31–36; 14.1–6; 18.37, 38
35	Pilate's Wife	Matthew 27.11–26
36	Herod	Luke 23.1–25
37	Barabbas	Mark 15.1–15
38	Pilate's Hands	Matthew 27.24–31; Isaiah 1.15–18
43	The First Crowd	Luke 19.35–40; 23.13–25
44	Simon of Cyrene	Mark 15.21; Romans 16.13; Philippians 2.5–11
45	The Second Crowd	Matthew 27.37–44; Psalm 22.15–18

46	Judas	Matthew 27.3–10; Acts 1.15–20
47	The Hierarchy	Mark 15.16–36
48	The Soldiers	John 19.23–37
49	The Thieves	Mark 15.32; Luke 23.39–49
50	You and I	Luke 23.24–38; 1 John 2.18–28
51	Pilate Writes	Matthew 27.37; Mark 15.26; Luke 23.38; John 19.19–22
52	Joseph	Matthew 25.31–46; 27.57–61
53	Nicodemus	Matthew 21.28–32; John 19.38–42
59	Peter and John	John 20.1–10; 21.3–11
60	Mary	John 20.11–18
61	'And Peter'	Mark 16.1–15
62	Thomas	John 20.19–31
63	Emmaus Walkers	Luke 24.13–35
64	Real People	1 Corinthians 15.1–19
65	Peter Again	John 21.1–19
66	John	John 21.20–25; 1 John 2.18–28
67	Five Hundred	Acts 1.1–3; 1 Corinthians 15.6; Matthew 28.16–20
74	Friend of Luke	Acts 1.1–3; Luke 1.1–4; John 15.12–16
75	Luke the Historian	Acts 1.1–14; Luke 3.1–3
76	Luke at Work	Acts 1.15–26; Psalm 69
87	The New Peter	Acts 2.1–36
88	The Converts	Acts 2.37–47
89	The Man at the Gate	Acts 3.2–11; John 9.8–25
90	Peter the Preacher	Acts 3.12–26; John 20.2–8
91	The Hierarchy	Acts 4.1–7; John 11.47–53
92	Peter's Courage	Acts 4.8–22
93	The Church in Jerusalem	Acts 4.23–37; 1 John 2.15–19; 3.13, 14

THE HOLY SPIRIT

Introduction

No subject, surely, can be of greater relevance to the situation in which we find ourselves these days than the doctrine of the Holy Spirit. The charismatic movement in all the denominations has emphasized the importance of the Spirit's work. It has also raised a number of difficult questions and we have come to see that the teachings of the Bible on this vital subject are all too little understood. If the truth be known, they are probably all too little studied. But in the New Testament the Spirit is constantly before us. He is constantly at work. It is not too much to say that it is impossible to live the kind of life the New Testament demands without the presence and the power of the indwelling Holy Spirit of God. This means that the study of the Bible's teachings about the Spirit must always be one of the Christian's absorbing preoccupations.

These studies are not meant to be controversial and the eager debater who is looking for fuel to help him carry on his disputes will, I fear, be disappointed. I have been concerned simply with what the Bible teaches. Of course, it is impossible for any writer not to have some views on current controversy, and I am not naïve enough to believe that I have escaped some bias in my treatment of controversial passages. But I have tried to avoid it and simply to let the Bible take me where it will.

The passages on which I was asked to comment take us through the significant teaching on the Spirit in both Old and New Testaments. They specifically relate His Person and work to those of the Son, and emphasize His connection with the growth of the Church and with the growth in grace of the believer. These are great themes and we cannot but be profited as we take seriously the teachings of such passages.

THE HOLY SPIRIT

A Divine Person

1 : Grieving the Holy Spirit
Isaiah 63.7–14; Ephesians 4.25–32

One of the difficult things in the interpretation of the Old Testament is the extent to which the Spirit is thought of as distinct from God the Father. In the case of a man, 'the spirit' and 'the man' are not two people. The two terms are not synonymous but we cannot say that two persons are involved. What is the position with God? Clear distinctions between the Persons of the Trinity are certainly found in the New Testament but the thought that the Spirit is a Person does not seem to have been developed in Old Testament times.

The Old Testament, however, does contain passages which indicate some kind of distinction within the Godhead. Expressions like 'the angel of his presence', 'the face of the Lord', or 'the name of the Lord' point to divine activity and are best explained in terms of something other than a unitarian understanding of the nature of God. In view of the fact that devout Jewish students, who take the whole Old Testament as divinely inspired, do not see the Spirit as separate in any way from the Father, we cannot say that the distinct personality of the Spirit is a necessary deduction from the Old Testament. But we can say that passages like Isa. 63 gain in force when we understand them in the light of the fuller revelation of the New Testament.

The prophet pictures God as loving and merciful (7). He has a deep and tender concern for His people and feels for them in their affliction. He saved them and redeemed them and 'carried them all the days of old' (9). It might have been expected that they would respond to this. But they did not. They rebelled. And they 'grieved his holy Spirit' (10). Now grief is something that we ascribe to persons only. It is meaningless to speak of a thing as 'grieved'. The Spirit is thus a Person, active and concerned for the people of God—One, moreover, who is deeply involved in their reaction to the divine leading. We ought never to think that

12

God is not greatly interested in the way we react to His good gifts. His Holy Spirit is grieved when we rebel.

So it is when Paul speaks of the kind of conduct that should characterize the Christian and goes on, 'do not grieve the Holy Spirit of God' (Eph. 4.30). Right through the Bible the Spirit of God is passionately concerned that God's people live as the people of God should. He is sharply opposed to all evil and is grieved when they give way to it. Hermas, a second-century Christian writer, calls the Spirit 'a cheerful Spirit' (using the Greek adjective *hilaron*, from which we get our word 'hilarity'). We should be clear that the Spirit is not a killjoy. And that we should avoid the kind of conduct that grieves this cheerful Person.

2 : The Spirit in the Church

Haggai 2.1-9; Acts 5.1-11

Theoretically, it would be possible to think of the Spirit as simply an influence, a force at work among the people of God and others. But the language used in both Old and New Testaments is such as to exclude this. The Spirit is not spoken of impersonally but in terms we naturally use of persons. Thus Haggai pictures the people after their return from the Exile, depressed and uncertain of themselves. They had undergone hardships and were doubtless wondering whether they had done the right thing in returning to the land of their fathers. The prophet encouraged them and they built the Temple of God which had fallen into ruins. Inevitably some who remembered the glory of the former building complained about the new one. In reply Haggai points out that in a very real sense the new Temple had a greater glory than the older one. That had been built by the wealthy Solomon and represented the generosity of a king who could well afford it. This new Temple was built by a people who were poor and without resource. It meant hard work and very real sacrifice. And this the Lord honours. Haggai puts the main emphasis of his encouragement on the fact that God is with the people. God says, 'I am with you' and again, 'My Spirit abides among you' (4 f.). The word translated 'abides' (literally 'stands') can indicate a permanent stay. We would not misinterpret it here if we translated, 'My Spirit lives with you'. It is this dynamic and living

13

Person who brings strength and inspiration to the dispirited Jews.

The well-known story of Ananias and Sapphira points a very different moral, but it likewise stresses the dynamic presence of a living Person. When Ananias told his lie in the presence of the church's representatives Peter spoke of this as a lie not to men, but to the Holy Spirit (3). The same apostle pointed out to Sapphira that her conspiracy with her husband was in fact an agreement to test out (so rather than 'tempt') the Holy Spirit (9).

The Spirit lives among people. He can be lied to. He can be tested out. How can we understand these things other than of a Person and a great divine Person at that?

3 : The Spirit Within

1 Corinthians 2

Paul has three important things to tell us about the Spirit in this chapter. First, effective preaching of the gospel is done in the power of the Spirit (4 f.). We ought never to think that it is great preaching or great organizing that brings men to Christ. God can, and does, honour such good works of His servants. But the gospel is powerful only when the Spirit of God is in it. It is the Spirit who speaks to the hearts of men, the Spirit who brings conviction of the truth of the gospel message, the Spirit who enables men to respond in repentance and faith.

The second point is that the Spirit is, so to speak, on the 'inside' of God (11). Paul uses the illustration of a man. Nobody knows what is going on inside a man. He may appear to be interested in an activity that is going on before him, while miles away in thought. From the outside another man can guess more or less accurately at the man's inner processes, but he cannot know them. Only 'the spirit of the man which is in him' really knows. In the same way it is only the Spirit of God who knows the thoughts of God. Men, especially spiritually-minded men, may guess at the ways of God. But they can know of them only what has been revealed. The Spirit's knowledge of God is different. He knows God from the inside and thus He knows God perfectly. Even the depths of God are open to His searchings (10).

The third point is that this divine Person, who knows God

14

from the inside, does not keep all this knowledge to Himself. He reveals some of it to men. The Spirit is given to men and He brings understanding of God's gifts (12). He teaches men the words to use (13) and He interprets spiritual truths (13). Paul is not talking about the insight possessed by the natural or un-spiritual man (14). He is talking about a God-given gift. All this can be no less than the working of a great divine Person who comes to men.

4 : The Spirit Sets Men Free

Romans 8.9–11; 2 Corinthians 3

It is of the utmost importance to be clear that the presence of the Spirit is not some optional extra to be found, so to speak, in the lives of super-Christians only. He is found in every believer and no one belongs to Christ unless the Spirit is in him (Rom. 8.9). This means more than a minor difference in non-essential matters. The Spirit's presence means radical revolution. So Paul speaks of the death of the body (Rom. 8.10), by which he prob-ably means an end to the power of what he elsewhere calls 'the body of sin' (Rom. 6.6, cf. 6.12; 7.24; 8.13). When a man comes to Christ the lower nature no longer dominates. Instead the Spirit of God transforms the man and makes him really alive. The life the believer has, he has because of the Spirit of God within him (Rom. 8.11).

It is this basic truth which enables Paul to speak of his Corin-thian friends as a letter written 'with the Spirit of the living God' (2 Cor. 3.3). The Spirit is not a minor influence, but is so domin-ant that their lives are a page 'written' by Him. This leads on to the thought that the whole Christian way is a way dominated by the Spirit. There is dispute as to whether Paul is specifically referring to the divine Spirit in his contrast with the letter, but none that it is the Spirit of God who gives the Christian life its peculiar power and special flavour. The presence of the Spirit transforms life and releases men from the bondage to the letter of the law that characterized the Jewish way.

There is further difficulty about 'the Lord is the Spirit' (2 Cor. 3.17). Some commentators (e.g. Tasker) think there is an explicit reference to the Holy Spirit. Others (e.g. Hughes) think it is Christ who is in mind. But none disputes that the life of which

Paul writes is a life enriched with the liberty the Spirit of God gives. 'Where the Spirit of the Lord is, there is freedom.'

Throughout today's passages, then, there runs the thought that the Holy Spirit is a Person who is concerned that men should live the fullest and freest of lives. When He comes into a man it is in order that that man be liberated and brought into the glorious experience of fellowship with God with all that that means in terms of power and liberty and joy. This cannot be less than the work of a divine Person.

5 : The Temple of God

1 Corinthians 3.16, 17; 2 Corinthians 6.14–7.1

In antiquity, temples were often built on a grand scale and they were usually richly adorned from the offerings of worshippers. Ordinary people lived in drab surroundings and the homes of the poor were shoddy. So they regarded their visits to temples as great occasions. In addition to being centres of worship, temples were places to meet people and often to transact a variety of business. But what characterized the temple above all else was that it was the home of the god. That was what gave it its special significance no matter what secular activities the worshipper might pursue there. It was his god's presence that governed his conduct when he was at the temple.

Paul has a revolutionary thought when he tells the Corinthians, not that they are in God's temple, but that they *are* that temple. Lest they miss the significance of what he is saying he underlines it: 'God's Spirit dwells in you' (1 Cor. 3.16). Just as a temple is set apart from all other buildings, so are Christians set apart from all other men (2 Cor. 6.15 f.). A temple is holy. It is to be used for no other purpose than the service of the god. The temple of the living God is no exception. Those in whom He lives must live as befits a temple. It is possible to regard the individual believer as a temple and sometimes the New Testament does this. But it is also possible to see the church, believers as a whole, as a temple, and that seems to be the case here, at least in ch. 3 (notice that 'temple' is singular while 'you' is plural).

'Do not be mismated with unbelievers' (2 Cor. 6.14) is often taken as referring to marriage. But Paul does not say this and we should see the passage as wider in application. It will have its reference to marriage. But Paul is saying that those who form God's temple must at all times behave accordingly. They will have contacts with non-believers, but they must beware of making of these such partnerships that their distinctive witness is compromised. Those in whom the Spirit lives must live as befits the presence of the Spirit whose characteristic designation is 'Holy'. So from another and a very practical angle we are reminded that we must see Him as a Person.

6 : Three Mighty Persons

Matthew 28.16–20; 1 Corinthians 12.4–6; 2 Corinthians 13.14

These three passages have in common that they all speak of God the Father, God the Son and God the Holy Spirit in such a way as to link them closely and to set them apart from everyone and everything else. We are so used to speaking of the Father, the Son and the Holy Spirit in this way that we do not stop to reflect that this is a curious procedure. We could not link anyone else in this fashion. We could not, for example, speak of the Father, the Son and the archangel Gabriel. This is not simply a matter of habit. It is incongruous to put anyone else there. No one, not even an archangel, fits. But every Christian recognizes the naturalness of putting Father, Son and Spirit together. The Father and the Son cannot be thought of other than as Persons and this implies that we should think of the Spirit in the same way. It would be very curious, to say the least, to associate two Persons and a force or influence.

The Matthean passage records our Lord's last appearance, when He gave His final command to the apostles. In it He charged them to evangelize 'all nations' in view of the fact that 'all authority' had been given to Him. Because of what He is they must proclaim Him throughout the world. But in making disciples and in baptizing them the apostles are not to think of Jesus as an isolated Being. In the act of baptizing they are to remember the place of the Father and the Spirit. Disciples are baptized in the name of the Spirit of God. From the beginning the Spirit is named upon them.

And this continues. Paul speaks of varieties of gifts and service, but of one God who gives the gifts and is the object of the service. And in the 'varieties of gifts' there is 'the same Spirit'

17

(1 Cor. **12**.4). As they engage in Christian service believers do not do so in their own strength. The gifts which enable them to serve are from the Spirit.

The 'grace' is familiar to us as a benediction. It speaks of the fellowship indwelt by, or created by, the Spirit. Either way it is the characteristic thing that the Spirit is there. Fellowship speaks of persons, and a fellowship that extends through the world and through the centuries speaks of a Person who is divine.

Questions and themes for study and discussion on Studies 1–6

1. Are there things in your life that grieve the Holy Spirit?
2. How may men lie to the Holy Spirit these days?
3. What are the implications for a Christian in today's world of the thought that the liberating work of the Holy Spirit is a work of God?
4. What does cleansing 'from every defilement of body and spirit' (2 Cor. **7**.1) mean for you?
5. How does the presence of the Spirit with believers everywhere help us understand His Person?

CHARACTER STUDIES

7 : Philip

John 14

We have observed the consistency through the New Testament in the characterization of the apostles. Philip has already appeared in the Gospel of John. He came from Bethsaida and was one of the first to be called. He was a friend of the devout and careful Nathanael, and appears to have been a man of somewhat similar character, knowing his mind, sceptical of the emotional approach, and seeking a certain basis of reason for projected action.

It is noteworthy that Philip was singled out by 'certain Greeks' who sought an introduction to Christ (12.20–23). Bethsaida, if the site is correctly identified, lay across the upper Jordan near its entry to the lake, and opposite Capernaum. It was the nearest lakeside Jewish town to the large Greek population of the Decapolis east of the lake. The Lord spent some time here, and it was here that the feeding of the five thousand took place. Perhaps here also is the key to the anxiety of Philip that the people be fed and his ready calculation of the magnitude of the task. They were his townsfolk (6.5–7).

Here too he had probably met Greek citizens from one of the Ten Towns which formed Decapolis, and may have been instrumental in stirring their interest in Christ. He is likely to have been, like his namesake in the Acts of the Apostles, more open to the ways and words of the Palestinian Greeks, than perhaps some of the other members of the group were. He was a ready evangelist as he showed at his call (John 1.43–46).

In this brief conversation Philip's longing for certainty produces one of the great words of Scripture. 'Don't carry that fear deep down in your hearts', says the Lord (1) 'believe in God and so believe in me.' 'Let us then see God,' cries Philip, with Moses' experience in mind (Exod. 33.12–23). The Lord answers with words which pick up the theme of 1.18—He, the Messiah, the Son of God, is God's demonstration of His invisible Person on earth, in terms which the human mind can understand.

Philip's reaction is not described. John is preoccupied with other matters. But here, for the mind's satisfaction, is the answer which cool minds like Philip's mind can grasp.

8 : The Branches
John 15

Chapter 14, you will note, ends with the words: 'Rise, let us go hence'. Chapter 18 begins with a reference to the departure for Gethsemane. Where, in the meantime were the actors in that night's tense drama? It is a fair guess that they were in the court-yard of Herod's Temple, in the headquarters of the foe, the last place where Judas and his band would be likely to look for them. They had left the Upper Room, to which he was likely first to come, with some abruptness. When the time was ripe they went to the Garden where he would surely next prosecute his search. In the meantime, they were safe, and the opening words of ch. 15 seem an indirect reference to the place of their concealment. He still had words to say.

Over the gateway of the Temple, carved in the white marble, was a vine. In the moonlight the gilded clusters, six feet long, would glitter gloriously. The disciples, countrymen all, were ever amazed at the mighty building on the hill, and it is easy to imagine their drawing their Master's attention to the sight, as they had earlier called to His notice the Cyclopean stones. It was ever His habit to link teaching to realities, and one can imagine the conversation. 'Master, see the great vine, see the moonlight on its carved fruit.' 'I am the true vine, you are the branches, and My Father is the vinedresser.' And pointing to the glow in the distant sky where the cuttings from the spring pruning burned in the Valley of Hinnom, He added solemn words of withered leaves and broken communion.

They, He said, were the branches. He meant that all who followed them in trusting Him, were also the branches. Here is where we become 'characters of Scripture'. The vine still has its enlivening sap. It still has its branches—those that bear richly the fruits of His Spirit, and those which lose their touch and wither.

9 : The Ordained
John 16

Look at ch. **15**, v. 16. The word 'ordained', the verb in the AV (KJV), is an inadequate translation. In modern English it is inseparable from the notion of ecclesiastical practice. At the time of its use by the translators it was no doubt an exact translation, for in Psa. **8** they spoke of 'the moon and the stars which Thou hast ordained.' The verb, in fact, meant, in the seventeenth century, 'set precisely in place'. It contained, if Psa. **8** is witness, the notion of astronomical accuracy. The Greek text asks for nothing more. It simply says: 'I have placed you that you should go and bring forth fruit.'

That statement covers the case of every Christian who truly seeks God's will. God promises in that word the employment of His perfect wisdom in the ordering and management of our lives. We are so 'placed' that fruitfulness must follow if we are prepared to accept the blessed fact that our circumstances are of God's ordering. No promise is made as to the nature of our place. For some it is prominence; for some it is obscurity: for some it is in the midst of all the activity commonly known as 'Christian work'; for others it is in apparent uselessness or unemployment, remote from all the tasks and offices of witness: for all it is God's best.

We, then, are the 'ordained', if we 'abide in Christ'. And, said Godet: 'Abiding is that continuous act whereby we lay aside all that which we might derive from ourselves to draw all from Christ by faith.' Let us leave circumstances to Him. He is preoccupied with what we are, not with what we can perform. His gospel, though committed to our hands, does not depend upon our hands. He cares first for our characters in Christ, for our spiritual fruitfulness. While, in the daily habit of surrender, He 'goes on increasing' all else will follow—'more fruit', 'much fruit'; and in that process other problems will find solution. All activity, each and every calling, any framework of trade, profession or business, is an opening and occasion for witness. The Christian presents his faith within the context of his daily life, but assuredly presents it more effectively, coherently, persuasively when study has sharpened his understanding, when a time of withdrawal, devotion and challenge has deepened faith and comprehension, and when reading and guidance have promoted maturity.

10 : The Sleepers

Matthew 26. 36–46; Luke 22.39–46

Gethsemane, the garden of the oil-press, for that is what the name means, lay across the Kidron, the stream whose ravine lies between the city walls and the Mount of Olives. Here the party went after the late hours spent in the Temple court. The men were worn out. It had been a tense and weary day. The emotions of the Supper, sensed but little understood, lay just beneath the surface of their thoughts. The puzzling words which occupy three whole chapters of John's Gospel had bewildered and wearied them. There was something about their Master which eluded their comprehension, something in the whole situation which gripped inexplicably at heart and mind. Wearied with grief and anxiety, they fell asleep under the gnarled olive trees. He had grown accustomed to loneliness these last days. The gap between Him and His men had opened on the Jericho road. It was wider still under the moon in the garden.

They slept. There is only Christ left for us to watch, and the sight is daunting. The agony in the Garden is one of the most awesome pages of Scripture. He was 'sore amazed', says Mark's account (14.33, AV [KJV]), using an unexpected word. What amazed the Son of God in this dreadful hour? Was it the depth of human evil which surrounded Him, the devastation Satan had wrought in the hearts of men, the depth of the abyss into which He knew He must step to achieve man's salvation? Was it the very pain of loneliness which amazed Him? It overwhelms the heart to think that God the All-sufficient yet craves the fellowship of man. 'The only-begotten Son, He has explained Him,' runs John 1.18, which we have more than once had occasion to quote, and the words must be taken to mean what they say. In a laudable desire to exalt God, some have removed Him far from man in splendour, sovereign might, and everlasting calm. And yet here was Christ, and Christ was God, seeking, in the hour of fierce pain, for the love and comfort of men. The solemn truth need not be evaded. God created man for Himself, and desires man's loyalty, fellowship and devotion, however inexplicable that wish may seem. We, too, can grieve the Lord by failing to 'watch with Him one hour' in the busy preoccupation of our days.

11 : The Youth in the Garden

Mark 1.1–8; 14.1–52

We have already seen that the cameo biographies of Scripture should not be neglected. We have met Enoch in an earlier volume. We shall meet Demas. Each has only a few words. All we know of Apollos is in a dozen verses. We have hardly any more for Mark, son of Mary, a widow of Jerusalem, nephew of the wealthy Cypriot Jew, Barnabas.

John Mark was the full name. John (Johanan) means: God is gracious, and was the boy's proper name. Marcus was his Gentile name, as Paul served for Saul, Jason for Joshua, Apelles for Abel, and so on. Mary's house, as we shall later see, was the meeting place of the Christian leaders. A maidservant is mentioned (Acts 12.13), but not Mary's husband, unless he was the man to whom allusion is made in 14.14. Perhaps he died soon after making his 'upper room' available for the Last Supper.

Imagination must play around the brief allusions if we are to form a picture of young Mark. Perhaps as a youth of fifteen or sixteen years he lay awake listening to the vague noises above, as the events of John 13 and Mark 14 took place. He might have sensed the tension which held the group that night, and felt the presence of danger. Listening and alert, he hears Judas descend the outside stairway, and perhaps recognizes him in the bright moonlight. Later there is the noise of many feet, and the rest depart.

Seizing a linen sheet from the bed, he rises and follows. Perhaps, lurking in the shadows, he heard the discourse of John 14, 15 and 16, and then, still keeping out of sight against the houses, followed the party to Gethsemane. There is a flare of torches under the olives, and the betrayer is there with the guards. With the reckless loyalty of youth, the boy shouts a protest, and angry hands lay hold of him. Perhaps this was the occasion of Peter's violence on the servant of the priest.

Mark slipped out of the linen sheet and fled, perhaps with a mutilating sword-slash across his fingers, for, in the early Church, Mark was the bearer of a nickname: 'the Stumpfingered'. Conjecture, no doubt, but the mysterious reference to the young man in the garden is in the fashion of an ancient signature. It is somewhat in the manner of a modern film producer, who makes a brief anonymous appearance in any film of his making. John 21.24 demonstrates similar anonymity.

Such is the first page of Mark's story. We shall meet him again, some fifteen years later, and we know him well in the terse, vivid pages of the Gospel he wrote for the Romans at Peter's request.

Questions and themes for study and discussion on Studies 7–11

1. 'He who has seen me has seen the Father' (John 14.9).
2. The use of imagery taken from farm and garden in the Bible.
3. Ordination in its modern meaning.
4. The meaning of 'watching in prayer' for us.
5. Loyalty and youth.

THE HOLY SPIRIT

Active in the Universe

12 : Creator Spirit
Genesis 1.1, 2; Psalm 33.6–9

The Bible associated the Spirit of God with this created universe right from the very first. The precise function of the Spirit, however, is not clear. The verb translated 'was moving' is not a common one, but it occurs again in Deut. 32.11 of the eagle fluttering over its young. The traditional Jewish way of understanding the passage has been that the Spirit of God 'hovered' over the waters like a dove (sometimes there is added, 'without touching them' or the like). Calvin thought the idea was that it was the Spirit who held together the watery chaos and made it stable. Many commentators maintain that the use of a term associated with a bird's care for its young introduces a note of tenderness and concern, and this is probably right. Kidner holds that the use of the term forestalls 'any impression of Olympian detachment' we might possibly derive from the later part of the chapter. He adds, 'this aspect of intimate contact must be kept in mind throughout.'

In Psa. 33.6 there is perhaps a reference to 'Spirit' in the word translated 'breath' (*ruach*). At any rate the psalmist is referring to the same creative activity as that in Gen. 1 where we have already seen reason for recognizing an activity of the Spirit of God. The Old Testament not infrequently associates the gift of life with the Spirit (e.g. Job 33.4; Psa. 104.30; Isa. 44.3 f.; Ezek. 36.26 f.). Here the psalmist is stressing the greatness of God who performed the work of creation so effortlessly. In the face of creation the only appropriate attitude on the part of created man is that of awe (8). When we realize what the Spirit of God has done we can only stand abashed. This reinforces the truth we saw in our first series of studies, that the Spirit is a great divine Person. And it emphasizes the other truth that the Spirit is not absent from any part of creation. He was involved in it from the first and He continues to be involved in it.

13 : The Breath of God

Genesis 2.4–7; Job 32.6–10; 33.1–7

There is a connection in Hebrew (as in many languages) between
'breath' and 'spirit'. Early man could not see or weigh breath.
But this invisible, intangible thing was necessary to life: when a
man ceased to have breath he ceased to live. It was the same with
the spirit of the man. That could not be seen or felt, but, however
it was understood, it was necessary to life. So the same word was
sometimes applied to the man's 'breath' as to his 'spirit'. In the
Old Testament *ruach*, 'spirit' (either a man's spirit or God's) may
also be translated 'breath' on occasion. Mostly, however,
'breath' renders *neshamah*, which was not normally used for
'spirit' (though cf. Job 26.4; Prov. 20.27). The two words, however, can come very close in meaning as we see from Elihu's
words, 'The spirit of God has made me, and the breath of the
Almighty gives me life' (Job 33.4). Here the parallelism shows
that the two expressions, 'the spirit of God' and 'the breath of the
Almighty', are similar in meaning. The statement underlines the
activity of the Spirit in creation and in the giving of life to men.
What we are we owe to the Spirit. And it shows that we must take
seriously statements about 'the breath of God' when we are
discussing the activity of the Spirit of God.

In Gen. 2 there is the story of how God formed man of dust
from the ground 'and breathed into his nostrils the breath of life;
and man became a living being' (7). It would be possible to take
this to mean that God caused the inanimate carcass to breathe,
and that that was what made it alive. But it is much more in
accordance with the Old Testament view of life and of 'the
breath of God' to see a reference to God's Spirit as putting the
'spirit' within man. It is the Spirit who gives life. Elihu seems to
take up this meaning, and even advance it a little, when he says
'it is the spirit (*ruach*) in a man, the breath of the Almighty, that
makes him understand' (Job 32.8). It is God's inbreathing that
enables a man to have understanding. Not only is the Spirit
responsible for life, but for life in its fullness.

14 : Life depends on God

Job 34.10–15; Psalm 104.24–30

To understand these two passages we must keep in mind the close connection in Hebrew between 'spirit' and 'breath'. It is as the Spirit of God gives living things breath that they live. Apart from this divine activity they must die. This is the point of Elihu's words in the Job passage. He sees God as just and as all-powerful. In the light of this he points out that if God were to take back 'his spirit' and gather 'his breath' all men would perish. 'His spirit' is not 'the Spirit of God' but the spirit in man that comes from the Spirit of God. In similar fashion the Preacher can describe death by saying 'the spirit returns to God who gave it' (Eccl. **12**.7). Were it not that God is active in man man would die. There is nothing in man that gives him inherent power over life. He lives only as God sustains him.

In Psa. **104** the psalmist is writing of the wonder of creation. He sees God's wisdom in all His works and he is especially struck by what he sees in life in and on the sea. Like Elihu he thinks of all of life as dependent on God. It is only as God gives the creatures food that they get it (28). And like Elihu he thinks of these creatures as dying when God takes their breath (or their spirit, *ruach*). This means returning to the dust, which will be a reference to their original creation out of dust (Gen. **2**.19). But unlike Elihu, the psalmist goes on to refer to the Spirit's creative work. Just as the withdrawal of the spirit or breath from the creature means death, so the presence of the divine Spirit means creative activity and life (30). It is important for us to be clear on the biblical view of the continuing activity of God in this universe. We should not see our world as something like a clock, which might be wound up, set going and left to run by itself. God is in His creation and without the sustaining work of His Spirit it must cease. We depend on God for the next breath we draw.

Employing Human Instruments under the Old Covenant

15 : The Skill of the Craftsman
Exodus 28.1–4; 31.1–11; 35.30–35

In recent times there has been an emphasis on the importance of secular life and scholars are writing books with titles like *The Secular Meaning of the Gospel*. This represents a reaction against a tendency on the part of some religious people to think of life as divisible into the sacred and secular. They saw things like worship and Bible study as activities where God's blessing might legitimately be sought and where the Spirit of God might be expected to be in operation. But the work of, say, a secretary or of a miner, was secular. The best that could be hoped for was that Christians in such occupations might do their work well and so make openings for the gospel.

Now we are realizing that we cannot divide life into two. All of life is God's. We serve Him just as really in our daily job as we do in our prayers, though the manner is different. Today's passages bring this truth out. The first of them makes it clear that the robes the priests were to wear as they went about the service of the tabernacle were not unimportant. The duly consecrated priests must serve God in the right way and the use of the robes God commanded was part of the right way (Exod. 28.1–4). Our traditional thinking might lead to the idea that 'spiritual' work began when the robes were worn. But not so. Bezalel was 'called' to the work of making these robes (others than ministers need a sense of vocation). And he was equipped by being 'filled . . . with the Spirit of God' (Exod. 31.1–3). Plainly the qualities set out in Exod. 31.3 ff. come from this gift of the Spirit and not any natural endowment. And equally plainly the gifts given to Oholiab and the other workers show that the same Spirit enabled them to do their work (Exod. 31.6 ff.; 35.34 f.; 36.1). This has important implications for every Christian as he works in his daily job.

16 : The Spirit and the Elders

Numbers 11.16, 17, 24–30

The Spirit's activity in inspiring the craftsmen to do their work
well was important. Less obvious, perhaps, but more important
was the way the Spirit enabled men to take their part in the
administration and government of the people. Moses occupied a
peculiar position. He was not exactly a king and it would be
difficult to say exactly how far his authority extended. But the
people certainly looked to him for leadership in a wide range of
their activities. Quite early he had trouble getting through his
many duties and his father-in-law advised him to delegate
responsibility (Exod. 18.13 ff.). But, though Moses heeded the
advice and appointed subordinate officials (Exod. 18.24 ff.), he
could still be in trouble and even complain to God about his
hard lot (Num. 11.11–15).

We may perhaps feel that the Lord's servant should not have
allowed himself to become irritated, even though we admit that
he had good cause for his irritation. But God did not blame him.
Instead, in His compassion, He made provision for the help that
His servant needed so much. He told Moses to gather seventy
elders who would share the responsibility and He promised that
He would 'put . . . upon them' some of the same spirit that Moses
had. Both in the promise and in the performance (17, 25) the
RSV has 'spirit' rather than 'Spirit', a choice which can be defended. But when they received this gift the men prophesied (25),
which makes it clear the gift must be thought of as a manifestation of the Spirit of God. It is important for us to see that
good administration is another facet of life in which God is
interested, interested enough, indeed, to put His Spirit on
seventy men so that they could perform this function adequately.
We must be on our guard against a sharp differentiation between
'spiritual' ministries, when prayer and preaching are prominent
and 'secular' ministries, when administration and the like are in
mind. Here, too, we need the Spirit. And the Spirit cannot be
contained. Joshua was jealous for Moses and thought Eldad and
Medad should be restrained. But the Spirit of God gives His
gifts with a lavish hand. There is no way of limiting them to a
few people, and we should not try. Moses shows us the more
excellent way (29).

17 : The Strength of Samson

Judges 13.24–14.20

After the two previous studies which showed that the skill of the craftsman and the excellence of the administrator may come from God it is no surprise to learn that the strength of the strong has, at least on occasion, been the result of an activity of the Spirit of God. In popular treatments of Samson far too much attention has been given to the hair of the strong man and not enough to what the Bible actually says. Three times in today's passage we are reminded that it was the Spirit of the Lord who moved him and enabled him to do what he did (**13.25; 14.**6, 19, cf. **15.**14). Samson was strong, not because he had long hair, but because he was the instrument of God to effect certain purposes. In the discharge of the tasks for which he was destined from the womb (**13.**3 ff.) strength was needed, and accordingly the Spirit gave him strength.

But we should notice two things about the Spirit's gift. One is that it was intermittent. The Spirit came upon Samson at different times, apparently to give him power for individual actions. The gift given to Christians differs in that the Spirit is a continuing endowment.

The other is that Samson was, in many ways, a curious recipient of God's good gift. In the incident in today's passage he does not appear in a very good light. We see him casually picking out a Philistine girl for his wife, defiling his Nazirite consecration by handling the carcass of a dead lion (cf. Num. **6.**6), entering a wager with thirty young Philistine men, and finding himself quite unable to resist the blandishments of his bride when she tried to worm his secret out of him. It is scarcely the record we expect from a man of God. Yet God did not withdraw His Spirit from Samson at this time; and even when He did, it was not permanent (cf. **16.**20, 28 ff.). We should not conclude that the way we live does not matter. It matters very much that we live up to all that is involved in our call to be the servants of God in our day and age. But the incident shows us that God does not desert His servants when they fail. He still works out His purposes. He still sends His Spirit to them.

18 : The Spirit and the spirits

1 Samuel 16

There are only two references to the Spirit of the Lord in this
chapter, those which speak of His coming on David and of His
leaving Saul (13, 14). But, though this is not said explicitly,
clearly it was the Spirit who enabled Samuel to see David as
God's choice. The Spirit then guided Samuel to David, came on
David for future service and left Saul who had departed from the
ways of God.

Samuel was impressed with Eliab and was quite ready to greet
him as the Lord's anointed. But the man on whom the Spirit
comes is not necessarily the man that men would choose. Eliab
was Samuel's choice, but he was not God's. When David was
marked out by the voice giving divine approval and by the
anointing which Samuel administered, the Spirit of the Lord
came mightily upon him. What this means is not explained. We
must take it in connection with the anointing to be king, which
means that in some way the Spirit of the Lord was preparing
David from that day forward for the service he was to render.

In sharp contrast is the statement that 'the Spirit of the Lord
departed from Saul' (14). This man had departed so far from the
ways of the Lord that the Spirit no longer equipped him for his
work as king. In our last study we saw that God does not withdraw His Spirit from us when our well-intentioned efforts go
astray and we slip into sin. But persistence in opposition to the
ways of God is incompatible with the presence of the Spirit of
God. In the last resort a man must choose to go God's way or
his own. Saul chose his own way and the Spirit departed from
him. We should probably connect with this the coming of the
'evil spirit from the Lord' that tormented him (14). The sacred
writer sees the hand of God in everything and thus even the
coming of this evil spirit had its place in the plan of God. It
does not mean that God refused to help Saul and deliberately
tormented him. But when Saul chose self instead of God, then in
this moral order that God has set up he invited a spirit of evil
to come to him. And it did. Our moral choices have far-reaching
consequences.

31

19 : Denouncing Evil

Micah 3.5–12

Knowing when the Spirit of God was speaking through a man
who claimed to be a prophet must have been a continuing problem
to the men of old Israel. They heard prophets like Isaiah or
Amos sounding out their 'Thus says the Lord' and recognized a
word from God. They did not pay prophets a salary but there
can be no doubt that they showed appreciation of what they
owed to these men of God by material gifts of some kind. But
then others appeared who also said, 'Thus says the Lord', e.g.
Zedekiah, the son of Chenaanah (1 Kings 22.11). Such men had
no word from the Lord, but how was the ordinary man to know
this? And, of course, unless they recognized them as false
prophets people would make the same gifts to such men as they
made to the prophets of God. With such prospects before them
the false prophets were irresistibly tempted to claim inspiration,
and to produce 'prophecies' that would please those who asked
(and paid!) for them.

It is this situation that Micah is facing. He denounces men
who have led people astray with their prophecies; prophecies
that were adapted to the gifts made to those uttering them (5).
Micah is able to assure such men that they will lack vision and
be disgraced (6 f.). How can he be so sure of this? Because the
Spirit of the Lord has filled him with power to denounce sin (8).
This is a tremendous advance on most of what we have seen in
our earlier studies. With no intention of depreciating gifts like
those of the craftsman or the strong man Samson, we can never-
theless say that ethical perception is much more important. And
Micah is assuring us that his knowledge of this evil is not something that he knows out of his own resources. He knows it only
because of the divine infilling. There was a constant idea in
antiquity that holiness and righteousness did not necessarily go
together. Men could be devoted to their god without becoming
better men and this attitude spilled over into Israel. But when a
man is filled with the Spirit of the Lord he has the insight to
recognize this for the evil thing it is and to denounce it. The
Spirit is concerned that men live uprightly. And if we have the
Spirit of God we will be concerned, too.

Questions and themes for study and discussion on Studies 12–19

1. What difference does the thought of the Spirit's 'intimate contact' (Kidner) make to our understanding of Genesis 1?
2. In what areas may we expect 'the breath of the Almighty' to give us understanding?
3. What does it mean for daily living that we depend on God for our very breath?
4. What are the implications for the modern Christian of Bezalel's being 'called' to work as a craftsman?
5. How far can we agree with the hymn writer who addresses the Spirit in the words,

   > *'I hate the sins that made Thee mourn*
   > *And drove Thee from my breast'* ?

6. Why is the Spirit characteristically called 'Holy'?

CHARACTER STUDIES

20: Annas
John 18.1–14; Psalm 22.1–13

It is not quite clear why Jesus was sent first to Annas, father-in-law of Caiaphas, the functioning high priest. The houses of the plotters of that night, Pilate and the hierarchy, were no doubt contiguous or near to each other, and Annas' family may, indeed, have occupied the same dwelling, so no great distance was involved.

Annas was a Sadducee, appointed by Quirinius in A.D. 7, and deposed by Valerius Gratus seven years later for presumptuously encroaching on a Roman area of jurisdiction. Cynically working on the Jewish assumption that a high priest was appointed for life, Annas continued to be the power behind the throne, a man of such influence and political acumen, that at various times he succeeded in securing the appointment to the high priest's office of five sons and a grandson, as well as Caiaphas, his daughter's husband.

The fact is testimony to the determination and the unscrupulous love of power which possessed the man. Edmund Burke once remarked that the possession of power, as nothing else, discovers with certainty what, at the bottom, is the true character of a man. It revealed Annas as a consummate villain. He was bitterly hated by the common people, but he would have agreed with a phrase quoted by Cicero from the lost tragedian Accius: 'Let them hate, provided they fear.' He was a man who enjoyed the reality of power, and cared little for its trappings.

On two counts Annas was determined to destroy Christ. The more personal reason was the twin assault on the cynical occupancy of the Temple courtyard by the notorious hucksters' market. Much wealth flowed into the hands of the hierarchy from this polluted source. And then, Annas, being in office in A.D. 7, must have been directly concerned in the establishment of the agreement with the Romans, hammered out on the deposition of Archelaus the year before. He and his wanted no one about who could form a centre for a 'king movement', or become a focus for Galilean demonstrations and rebellion. In this he found himself in agreement with Pilate, anxious for a quiet Passover. That it meant the death of a good man did not enter into consideration. Tacitus was to write before the end of that century: 'Power acquired by guilt has seldom been directed to a good end or useful purpose.'

21 : Caiaphas

John 11.47–57; Exodus 23.1–8

Caiaphas, Joseph Caiaphas as Josephus his namesake calls him, bore a responsibility greater than any other person on a judge's bench has ever borne. We know little enough about this villain. He became high priest under Valerius Gratus in A.D. 14, and was deposed by the Governor of Syria, Lucius Vitellius, in A.D. 36, immediately after Pilate's recall to Rome. Perhaps both careers ended in the same context of circumstances.

Caiaphas was therefore in office when Pilate came to Palestine in A.D. 26, and held power all through the period of the procurator's term. He must have had a difficult task in view of Pilate's shocking relations with the Jews. Such matters played their part in a despicable and designing mind when the menace (or so he regarded it) of a new religious movement arose from the turbulent district of Galilee.

Caiaphas is a not uncommon phenomenon of life and history —a man of low character in a high position. In religion he found, not a way of life, but a career. All he truly believed in was himself. It was La Fontaine who remarked well three centuries ago that 'anyone entrusted with power will abuse it, if he is not also animated with love of truth and virtue, whether he be a prince or whether he be a man of the people.'

There is in fact no difference. Vice is common to all ranks of society. Evan John Simpson once put it into verse as he watched the crowd in the lounge of a Jerusalem hotel in wartime. He could see the universal types of sin:

> *Herod from Egypt with corn and with cotton*
> *Held from the children till prices increase,*
> *Young Pontius Pilate with gleaming Sam Browne,*
> *Sipping pink gin as he passes the buck:*
> *'I've washed my hands of it, turned the job down,*
> *'Tisn't my pidgin, if things come unstuck . . .'*

35

Oh, you who felt the blood, the nails, the blows,
Pardon us now, as once you pardoned Rome
And breathe on us who have forgotten you
Your ancient peace—'They know not what they do.'

Caiaphas, perhaps, deserved no such charity. He knew what he did, and did it all the same. And yet, perhaps, he knew a life of gall and wormwood. It is significant that Annas, deposed though he was, is called high priest in Acts 4.6. The Jews looked on the office as lifelong. Caiaphas held his position by Rome's sanction. Hence the humiliation of having his father-in-law called by his title.

22 : The False Witnesses

Matthew 26.57–68; Deuteronomy 19.16–20

Jewish law, both as laid down in the Mosaic code and in the Mishnah, the corpus of law composed by the Rabbis from their oral traditions, was extremely careful on court procedure. There were clear directions laid down regarding the testimony of witnesses. Those giving evidence were admonished before the court and then put out and heard separately one by one. Only if they were found to agree together were the judges to consider their evidence.

The criminals who bore witness against the Lord did not fulfil this condition. They disagreed among themselves and should have been dismissed for the scoundrels they were. They must have been bribed denizens of the streets, chosen rather for their unscrupulous disregard for the truth than for any other quality. Caiaphas and his associates in the night's crime touched a new low level of evil when they found it necessary to associate their cause with such allies. It is difficult to see into minds so darkened. The solemn penalties laid down in the Mosaic ordinances against the crime of false witness, make it clear that only men who had abandoned all good could be induced to utter such falsehood— and against such a one.

Again, the type has not departed from our midst. False witness is still brought forward against Christ. His presence haunts the world and challenges conscience, and if some can diminish Him, misrepresent Him or distort Him, they undertake the task in an effort to dismiss Him. And if 'this is the way the Master went, should not the servant tread it still?'

Lies and misrepresentation are evil's favourite weapons against good. It should not astonish the Christian to find his words subtly twisted and quoted out of context, to find action and motive misconstrued. To tell the truth about the good exalts it, and if evil would be rid of good and bring it down, it must necessarily use falsehood to discredit and destroy. The forms and process of a fine judicial system were perverted to this end. It was expedient, the rulers had decided, to be rid of the disturbing presence of Christ. Caiaphas had said as much, in words to which history was to give an awesome twist (John 11.49–53). In lowest hypocrisy they employed the instruments of justice to this end.

23 : Peter

John 18.15–27

Sadly enough, there are more ways of bearing false witness to Christ than lying about Him. Somewhere into the passage prescribed from Matthew's Gospel yesterday, must be fitted John 18.19–21. It runs literally, though few of the English translations do it justice: 'Therefore the high priest asked Jesus about His disciples.' Unable to see how 'therefore' can refer to Peter's loud denial by the coal fire in the courtyard, Moffatt at this point makes one of his unjustified transpositions which so mar his translation.

The verse means what it says. From the story of the examination of the blind man in John 9, it appears that proceedings in the hall where the Sanhedrin met were visible and audible from the courtyard. John, who for some reason had access to the high priest's house, must have heard the debate from that vantage-point and so reported it. Peter's denial was audible both to Caiaphas, who was conducting the inquisition, and to the Prisoner.

The case was going badly. The witnesses were contradicting each other. The Sadducee was becoming desperate. Then he became aware of a disturbance by the brazier in the courtyard and a distinctly Galilean voice loud in denial. Caiaphas was no fool. Here was an opportunity. '*Therefore* he asked Jesus about His

37

disciples.' Knowing that Peter could hear Him, Jesus replied that He had made no secret of His teaching. Many had heard all He had to say. 'Ask them,' He concluded.

It could have been Peter's finest hour. He could have accepted the dual challenge, stepped forward and denied that his Master said anything blasphemous or seditious. He was silent. The company beside the coal fire had been too much for him. It is well for us to see a symbol here. To seek comfort by the world's coal fire can be harmless enough provided we are sturdy enough in character to withstand the confrontation of those who share the place. Comfort should have no priority, if compromise or breakdown is too large a temptation there.

Christ Jesus has one vulnerable point when the hostile world seeks to discredit Him. No truth prevails against Him. False witness of the baser or more blatant kind, from 'rationalist' argument to crude rock opera has no ultimate power to harm Him. His vulnerable point is His fallible disciple—I or you. Luke (22.61) reports a poignant phrase: 'The Lord turned and looked straight at Peter . . .' In the act of betrayal they are difficult eyes to meet.

Questions and themes for study and discussion on Studies 20–23

1. Power as a revealer of character.
2. Caiaphas and Pilate in today's world.
3. 'False witness', conscious and unconscious.
4. 'The world's fire of coals.'

THE HOLY SPIRIT

Preparing for the Messiah's Advent

24 : The Spirit of Wisdom
Isaiah 11.1–9

The idea of anointing is important throughout the Old Testament.
It marked certain men out for special service, e.g. the king ('the
Lord's anointed') or the priest ('the anointed priest'). But as the
men of the Old Testament saw the inadequacies of the best of
God's servants, and as they contemplated the greatness of the
task men of God should be doing, they were led by the Holy
Spirit to look for the coming in due time of One who would
be specially important in God's working out of His will. This One
would be not 'an' anointed, but 'the' anointed, or, to use the
technical term, the Messiah. This is our transliteration of the
Hebrew word meaning 'anointed' (translated into Greek it becomes *Christos* from which we get 'Christ'). The term itself does
not often occur, but the idea is widespread in the Old Testament.

In today's passage we learn that the Messiah will be a descend-
ant of Jesse (David's father; i.e. he would be of Davidic stock).
Immediately, the prophet goes on to the thought that the Spirit
of the Lord will 'rest upon him'. The Spirit came upon Jesus as
He commenced His mission (Mark 1.10). While there are not
many references to the Spirit during the ministry of our Lord, the
general impression the Gospels leave is that the Spirit rested upon
Him throughout His earthly life, as later studies will show. In
other words we see in the Gospels the fulfilment of what is here
foreshadowed. The Spirit was the essential equipment of the
Messiah.

Included among the gifts that the Spirit will bring are 'wisdom',
'understanding', 'counsel' and 'knowledge'. While distinct these
are clearly related and they indicate the importance of *ideas* in
Messiah's work. Earthly power is not important, as we see from
Jesus' ministry. He never accepted the current view that the
Messiah would win a military triumph over the Romans. Yet the
Spirit did give Him 'might', power in the spiritual realm which
we may not unfairly connect with 'the fear of the Lord', which

ensured the completion of the programme envisaged in today's passage. Nobody can resist Him as He implements the heavenly wisdom. The Spirit of the Lord sees to it that the true wisdom and not some merely earthly knowledge is at work in the messianic programme. In the modern confusion this still bears thinking about.

25 : The Servant of the Lord

Isaiah 42.1–4; 61.1–4

The Servant of the Lord is a great figure in certain poems in the latter part of the prophecy of Isaiah. When we read these, especially Isa. 52.13–53.12, we are usually taken up with the way in which they set forth the atoning ministry of our Lord. This must always be of absorbing interest to God's people, but it is worth noticing also that there are passages, like those now before us, which bring out the place of the Spirit in the work of the Servant. As we saw in our last study, the Spirit came on Jesus as He began His ministry. Now we see something of what that means.

In the first passage the emphasis is on the discouraged and the defeated, the 'bruised reed' and the 'dimly burning wick'. In ancient Palestine reeds and wicks were cheap and plentiful. For most people it was not worth persisting with a defective example of either. Simpler by far to throw it away and start again. But the Spirit-filled Servant of the Lord does not do this with damaged lives. He does not act as the world does, He saves them and persists to final victory. And this is right. It means justice as well as mercy (42.1, 4). There is guidance here for the servants of the Lord as they engage in their lesser ministries.

There is a peculiar interest in Isa. 61, for Jesus Himself chose to use these words when He spoke about His own ministry. After reading the opening part of our passage in the synagogue at Nazareth, He said to the people, 'Today this scripture has been fulfilled in your hearing' (Luke 4.21). The reference to anointing (61.1) seems to show that what follows is the messianic task: our Lord's use of the passage makes this sure. The Spirit anointed Him for the work that He was to do throughout His ministry. The 'good tidings' Jesus preached was not a message of human origin, but one due to the Spirit's anointing. Right through the passage there runs a deep concern for the afflicted. The gospel is not a message for the comfortable, but for those in trouble. For such the Spirit-filled Messiah has a message. His saving work makes good 'the devastations of many generations' (61.4).

26 : The Transforming Spirit

Isaiah 32.9–20; 43.25–44.5

In both today's passages there is a contrast between the tragic consequences of sin and the vigorous life the Spirit of God gives. Consistently the Old Testament teaches that when men sin punishment follows. It is not always immediate, but it is sure. The truth is illustrated over and over again in the history of the chosen people. In accordance with this Isa. 32.9–14 has a striking picture of complacent Israel and of the inevitable consequence of Israel's sin. In this case the disaster is forecast in little more than a year (10). God's punishment will be seen in the failure of the agricultural processes (10) with the consequent desolation of both city and countryside (14). Later the prophet speaks of God's punishment of the evil of other nations (43.14). We should be clear that, while men may sin for a time with impunity, in the end sin always pays its wages.

But the emphasis in both our passages is not on sin and its ill deserts, but on God's good gift in sending the Spirit. When the Spirit is poured out there will be effects in nature (32.15), but even more in moral qualities—justice, righteousness, peace, quietness and trust. In days like our own there is need for stress, first on the fact that these things come as the result of God's good gift, not man's endeavour, and secondly that it is not peace that comes first but justice and righteousness. Peace is the effect of righteousness (32.17), not a good that can be obtained quite apart from righteousness.

Though all this was held out to the Israelites of old, in fact, the prophet saw that the men of his day would not yield to the Spirit and find the blessing. So he spoke of Him as coming on their descendants (44.3). We notice two things of importance. First, God does not go back on His purpose or His promise. The word is expressly addressed to Jacob and to Israel (44.1). Secondly, the full outpouring of the blessing awaited the coming of the Messiah. It was only as the result of His saving work that men received the Spirit in His fullness.

41

27 : The Vindication of God

Ezekiel 36.22–38; 39.25–29

The Exile was one of the great pivotal events of Israelite history. The Old Testament leaves us in no doubt about the shattering effect it had on the nation. Before it some had thought comfortably that in the last resort God must intervene to save His people, as He had done when Sennacherib threatened (2 Kings 19.35 f.). After it they knew that God viewed sin as so serious that He was quite capable of allowing their enemies to triumph over them when they sinned.

Today we are concerned with the vindication of God in the transformation of His people. The prophet points out that, in what had happened, God's name was profaned among the nations (36.23). This would not be allowed to continue. God would bring His people home. But He is a moral God and He would not bring them back simply in order that they might resume their old sinful practices. So He speaks of cleansing them from their idolatry (36.25). The worst thing about the people, however, was not their outward worshipping of idols but their inward state of heart and spirit. So God says that He will give them 'a new heart' and put 'a new spirit' in them (36.26). This might be taken to mean that God would enable them to look at life in a different spirit. But the word from God proceeds, 'I will put my spirit within you' (36.27), and this should surely be taken to mean 'the Spirit of God'. It was necessary that the people make a clean break with sin and that they live lives honouring to God. But they had showed over and over again that they were quite unable to do this. They needed a strength not their own. What God now says to them is that that strength will be given them. His own Spirit will come into them and He will enable them to live as they never could have lived left to themselves. They will be able to observe God's commandments (36.27) and turn from evil (36.31). Our second passage carries the same basic message and it culminates in the promise of the pouring out of God's Spirit (39.29).

There is a sense, of course, in which all this took place at the return from the Exile. But the fulfilment then was at best partial. Really to put away sin was the work of the Lord Jesus, and the fullness of the Spirit's indwelling was the fruit of His work.

28 : The Spirit and All Flesh

Joel 2.15–32

The call to repentance (15–17) is followed by the announcement of the Lord's blessing (18–27). The sequence is important. The blessing of God is not a gift given without regard to ethical and moral considerations. A dallying with sin and the indwelling of the Spirit do not go together, which perhaps explains some of the powerlessness in the modern Church. But when sin is grieved over and put away the way is prepared for the coming of God's Spirit. Joel speaks of all manner of blessings as he leads up to the Spirit. But repentance is the prerequisite of them all.

He looks for the coming of the Spirit at some future time ('afterward', v. 28). God says that He will pour out the Spirit 'on all flesh'. This does not mean on every member of the human race without distinction, but it does mean that the Spirit will not be restricted to a select few. In our earlier studies we have seen how the Spirit came upon outstanding individuals and equipped them for unusual work. But in the time of which Joel speaks all God's people will receive the Spirit. He goes on to the results. 'Your sons and your daughters shall prophesy' removes any distinction of sex. There is similarly no distinction between old and young. We should probably not put a difference between dreaming dreams and seeing visions. Poetic parallelism makes these much the same and neither differs greatly from prophesying. All are ways in which God reveals His will. It is most interesting that 'the menservants and maidservants' (i.e. slaves) are included among those receiving the Spirit, for, in antiquity, most people would not have seen these lowly folk as suitable recipients of God's great gift. But God's Spirit is for all God's people without distinction.

We should not take the 'blood and fire and columns of smoke' literally, for Peter claimed the fulfilment of this prophecy at the day of Pentecost (Acts 2.16–21). They are part of the picture. Verses 30–32 make it clear that the outpouring of the Spirit spoken of ushers in the messianic age. The work of Messiah and the gift of the Spirit go hand in hand.

*29 : The Forerunner

Luke 1.13–17, 39–45

We have seen that in Old Testament days the Spirit did many things in preparation for the coming of the Messiah. It is not surprising accordingly to find Him at work in John the Baptist, who was to be the immediate forerunner of the Lord. John's birth was unusual in that both his parents were 'advanced in years' (Luke 1.7). But not only was his conception unusual, the child was to have an unusual gift of the Spirit right from the womb (15). Following on this we are told of his special task. This is described in various ways and summed up in the words, 'to make ready for the Lord a people prepared' (17). The clear implication is that the preparation of a people for the Messiah was a task that needed the special equipment of the Holy Spirit. It could not be done on the merely human level. The interesting thing is that while the Spirit was to fill John the Baptist the emphasis is not on that great prophet, but on Messiah who would come.

It is the same with our second passage. Elizabeth was filled with the Spirit when she met Mary. As a result she uttered a little poem (it is printed as prose in the RSV, but it is really poetry). In it she does not exult in the son who is to be born of her, as might have been expected. In fact she does not mention him except as he leaped in her womb to greet his Lord. It is Mary's son on whom the Spirit-filled Elizabeth concentrates. So she pronounces Mary blessed, clearly because of the Son she was to bear. She goes on to speak of Him as 'my Lord' and to interpret (under the Spirit's leading) the movement of the babe in her own womb as a leaping for joy at the approach of the mother of the Lord. We see the same thing in the song of Zechariah (Luke 1.68–79), a song uttered when the old priest was filled with the Holy Spirit. His first words after receiving back his speech were not a celebration of his personal relief, nor a thanksgiving for his own small son, but a thanksgiving for God's sending His Messiah. The Spirit centres on the divine action for all mankind.

*30 : The Glory and the Gloom

Luke 2.22–35

Simeon comes before us only in this incident. He is usually
thought of as an old man, but Luke does not say this. He was
both righteous (i.e. he did his duty towards men) and devout (and
that towards God). But what distinguished him from other
people was that 'the Holy Spirit was upon him' (25).

It was the continuing presence of the Spirit with him that made
him so outstanding. As we have seen, under the old dispensation
the Holy Spirit came on people for special occasions, but a
continuous presence of the Spirit was rare. Clearly Simeon was an
unusual man, and one who lived very close to God.

One specific revelation the Spirit had made to him was that
he would see the Christ of God before he died. Thus his presence
in the Temple when Joseph and Mary came to make the prescribed
offerings (Exod. 13.2, 12, 15; Lev. 12.1–8; Num. 18.15 f.) was
not accidental. It was God's providential way of accomplishing
the fulfilment of His promise. Simeon celebrated the occasion
with a little song which has been greatly loved and greatly used
by generations of Christian worshippers. In it he refers to God's
'salvation' by which he means the Child through whom, in due
course, God's salvation would be accomplished. This would
have its effects on both Gentiles and Jews. The link of revelation
with Gentiles and glory with Israel should not be pressed. Both
gifts will come to both groups though there is special fitness in
linking glory with Israel in view of the importance of the concept
in the Old Testament.

Simeon went on to notice something of what this would mean.
The 'fall and rising' may mean that people must become
humble before they can be exalted, or it may point to a division
on account of Christ, those who accept Him being raised, while
those who reject Him fall. This salvation will not be purchased
without cost. The Spirit-inspired Simeon goes on to refer to the
'sword' that will pierce Mary's soul. The imagery is vivid. The
cross will mean suffering for Mary as well as for Jesus. This
prophecy, with Jesus still a baby, underlines the purpose worked
out in the cross. That was the way God had always planned to
save men. But it needed the inspiration of the Spirit for this to
be seen.

31 : John's Witness to the Spirit

John 1.19–34

Only one thing is recorded about John the Baptist in the Fourth Gospel; he bore witness to Jesus. The increasing curtness of his answers to the questions in the first part of our passage is connected with this. He wanted to bear witness to Jesus and these people kept asking him questions about himself. But he did manage to do what he aimed at and pointed men to the greater than he, whose sandal he was not worthy to untie (26 f.).

He speaks of Him as 'the Lamb of God' and then goes on to bear further witness. He saw the Spirit come down from heaven like a dove (32). The reason for this imagery is not known. The dove was not, as is often said, a symbol for the Spirit (it became so among the Christians as a result of reflection on this passage and the parallels; but it is not found previously). It was sometimes used for Israel and perhaps we are to think of the reception of the Spirit as marking Jesus out as the true Israelite. And not only did the Spirit come down on Jesus, but He 'remained on him' (32), a detail not in the other Gospels. This points to a permanent endowment.

When John goes on to say that he did not know Him, it is uncertain whether he means that he did not know Jesus at all (which is possible; although related to Him, he had been brought up in the wilderness, Luke 1.80), or that he did not know that He was the Messiah. Either way, it was the descent of the Spirit that brought conviction. He had been given a sign and knew that the One on whom the Spirit came was the Messiah. Again we see the importance of the Spirit for Messiahship.

And we see something further, for John goes on to say that the revelation made to him included the information that Messiah is 'he who baptizes with the Holy Spirit' (33). It is through Jesus that men are brought into vital contact with the Spirit of God. The figure of baptism stresses abundant supply. The Spirit is given with no grudging hand. There is a quality of life that Christ makes available for men and which is characterized by the continuing presence of the Spirit of the living God.

Questions and themes for study and discussion on Studies 24–31

1. What do you see as the importance of the gifts of Isa. 11.2 in the light of the present day?

2. What relevance has the Spirit's concern for justice (Isa. 42.1, 4) to your situation?
3. How far can we apply the words of Isa. 32.17 to the modern world situation?
4. What is the importance of the gift of the Spirit to slaves?
5. John the Baptist's task required him to be filled with the Spirit. Do you see this as the general rule?
6. Reflect on the importance of John's emphasis on the fact that the Messiah would baptize with the Holy Spirit.

CHARACTER STUDIES

32 : The Procurator
Luke 13.1–3; Acts 3.12–19

A procurator was a minor governor, responsible directly to the emperor. The name means 'manager' or 'steward', and such officers were used in difficult and dangerous areas, where the emperor desired direct contact with events. Hence an element of urgency in Pilate's position.

Pontius Pilate, procurator of Judea, is known almost as well as any Roman of the first century. He stands full length in the four small books which tell the story of the trial of Christ. A baffled and frustrated man, neatly netted by the subtle priests in the web of his past follies, arrogance and compromise, Pilate is both victim and villain in the Easter story. He betrayed Roman justice, and he betrayed it because he was a coward, unwilling to pay the price of courage. He could not afford another appeal to Caesar. Twice the clever priests had already challenged his rule, and made him pay for an act of folly. It is not uncommonly the experience of men that the price of moral dignity and uprightness rises with each failure to claim it as a human right.

So it was that the procurator of Judea was driven into the crime, the gravity of which he was quite conscious of, and found a place of scorn in history. He would have had a minor place apart from his fatal confrontation with Christ. He appears twice in the pages of Josephus, the Jewish priest who became the Emperor Vespasian's secretary and used his leisure time to write a detailed history of his people. He appears briefly in the writings of Philo, the Jewish scholar of Alexandria. And in all these non-biblical contexts he shows the same hard face, cruel, foolishly contemptuous of the difficult people he was called to rule. He was a bad appointment for the enormous task of holding the peace with a garrison of only three thousand men, in a country where the heat of rebellion and frustrated nationalism was daily rising. Above all, his task was to keep peace in an area of turbulence behind a difficult and sensitive frontier. Old Tiberius, in grim and silent retirement on Capri, was no person with whom to trifle. Pilate could have outfaced the Jewish plotters, had past misrule not betrayed him into their hands. Ultimately, the price of evil must always be paid.

33 : The Judge
John 18.28–40; Luke 23.1–7

This is a revealing passage. The accusers would not enter the Gentile judgement hall for fear of ritual pollution—they who were murdering a man. Pilate came out to them and asked the formal question which opened a Roman trial (29). It was the question they might have expected, and any accuser, knowing that such a query always initiated proceedings, would have been ready with the formal indictment. These men were experienced in such procedure. Why then were they not ready with a formal reply to a formal and customary question? Their documents should have been in their hands.

They answered in blank amazement. 'We would not have brought him to you, were he not an evil-doer.' This was no reply. Pilate was a judge, not an executioner. Why did they not treat him as a judge, and make their accusation? The only explanation which fits the facts casts an ill light on the character of all the participants. They expected, not a trial, but the signing of the death warrant. They expected no legal exordium, no question at all, no waste of time.

And why could they be sure that a magistrate of the occupying power, a trained judge and servant of Tiberius, would thus dispense with the formalities of justice? They had no right to expect such informality, save under one set of circumstances. Pilate must have given an undertaking that he would not conduct a formal trial, but hand the Prisoner over, on the word of the priests, to the execution squad. There must have been a discreditable understanding.

There is a chapter missing from the story. Caiaphas and Annas, or one of them, must have been in conclave with the procurator the night before, and by some form of cajolery, menace or subtlety, secured a promise that a trial would be by-passed. And why then, when thus presented with the occasion he had been led to expect, did Pilate change his mind, and, fighting for time, slip into the lifelong habit of the bench, and open the proceedings, to their indignant amazement, with the formal expression of 'the

Accusation'? Perhaps Matthew's story gives a clue, and to that
we will soon turn.

*34 : Pilate and Truth
John 8.31–36; 14.1–6; 18.37, 38

On this high-lifted stage words and events assume cosmic
significance. John was an eye-witness of the trial, and he it was
who caught up Pilate's despairing remark about the truth. 'What
is truth?' he said with an angry frustrated shrug of the shoulders,
and strode off to tell the Jews that he found no fault in the
Prisoner. He had, in fact, confronted the truth. It even found a
lodgement on his lips. All he needed for salvation was to act
upon it.

Francis Bacon, in opening his famous essay on Truth, mis-
interpreted Pilate. 'What is truth? said jesting Pilate; and would
not stay for an answer.' Pilate was in no jesting mood. He had a
touch of the modern academic about him. He despaired of
absolutes. In the modern world, he might have sloughed off the
superstition which allowed his wife's dream to disturb him. He
would have fallen easy victim to the cult of the suspended judgement, the perpetual and unsatisfied enquiry into the exact
significance of words, and that habitual dismissal of all which
lacks the senses' proof as 'meaningless', the habit which makes
faith so difficult for those who succumb to certain types of
education.

'It is heaven upon earth,' says Bacon later in his essay, 'to
have a man's mind turn upon the poles of truth.' And it is no
comfort to have it swerve and oscillate on doubt. 'I am the truth.'
Christ said, not long before the morning of Pilate's question. By
that He meant that His presence sets much in perspective, informs
the moral judgement on which so much of life depends, and lays
a groundwork for a plan of purposeful living.

But return to Pilate's 'moment of truth'. To the Jews waiting
impatiently outside his judgement hall, he proclaimed in downright words the innocence of the One they had brought for
condemnation. There is no fit search after the truth which does
not begin with the truth it knows. Pilate had a pathway from that
one clear realization to salvation. No further truth becomes
manifest to man unless the truth he knows is accepted and fused

with thought and being. 'It is not enough,' said Coleridge rightly, 'that we swallow truth. We must feed upon it as insects do on the leaf, till the whole heart be coloured by its qualities, and show its food in every fibre.' Pilate had his opportunity. The answer to his question lay down that path.

*35 : Pilate's Wife

Matthew 27.11–26

Was it Pilate's wife who caused Pilate, in the midst of his plot with the Jews, to change his mind? The whole incident rings with truth. Governors of provinces were frequently accompanied by their wives. Tacitus describes an attempt made by the Roman Senate to put down the practice, which was completely unsuccessful. Pilate, too, was a man who stood in frequent need of counsel.

One tradition has it that he was a member of the College of Augurs, a contention borne out by the device on one of his coins —a *lituus*, or priest's staff. As such he would be interested in the interpretation of omens, and a dream was ominous material of the first order.

Consider, too, the psychological likelihood of the narrative. Was Pilate's wife present or within hearing when he made his disgraceful bargain with the priests? She obviously knew enough about the Lord to have formed her own most definite conclusions about Him. He was 'a good man'. She must have known that crime was afoot, and that her husband was lending himself, contrary to all Roman justice, to its consummation. She was ashamed of him, and no woman cares to be ashamed of her husband. Nor, with such a woman, would pleas of expediency avail.

She went to rest with these preoccupations gnawing at her mind. Dreams are normally made out of the stuff of the day's experience, especially of its fears and its frustrations. She dreamed some frightening and disturbing dream, woke before dawn to find her husband gone, remembered the pre-dawn meeting corruptly arranged between Pilate and the hierarchy, and in haste wrote a swift brief note to try to save her husband from his crime and folly. Conjecture, to be sure, but the story hangs together, for what that is worth.

51

Conjecture aside, all that which cold factual history knows about this woman is contained in one verse (19). Apocryphal literature and tradition have played with the theme, and Claudia Procula, as she is thus named, along with the man she tried to save, is honoured by the Greek and Coptic churches. It is a pity that we do not know more. Pilate's wife, on the brief evidence of the one verse, must have been a remarkable woman. What were the 'many things she suffered' in her dream? Hers is the first Roman tribute to Christ recorded in history.

36 : Herod

Luke 23.1–25

We move from narrative to narrative as the story builds itself before us. Could there be more striking evidence of all absence of collusion between the authors as we discover one detail here and another there? The interview with Herod is mentioned only in Luke. Pilate was seeking in desperation to avoid administration, and he laid hold of the slender pretext that the Prisoner was a Galilean, and therefore under the jurisdiction of the king.

Herod was in Jerusalem, where he had a residence, for the Passover. He observed such formalities as part of his precarious dual policy—safe and impeccable relations with both the Romans and the Jews. Herod was 'glad to see Jesus'. He expected perhaps some demonstration of extraordinary psychic power from Him. There is an odd phrase in the account (9). Literally it runs: 'He questioned Him with words enough.' It was evidently a determined cross-examination, with the doomed kinglet, so accustomed to the petty sycophancy of his small court, unable to extract a word from the silent person who had now nothing to say to him. It was Jesus' silence, perhaps, which prompted the other evangelists to omit the story of the visit to Herod. Luke saw its significance.

There comes a time in the experience of a determined evil-doer when the process of evil becomes irreversible. The Lord spoke of this solemn fact to the Pharisees, as we have earlier seen. There is a sin against the Holy Spirit, a sin unpardonable, and physical life can continue past the moment of spiritual death, which the final commission of this sin represents. 'My Spirit shall not always strive with man', runs an awesome saying, and God had ceased to strive with Herod. He made his choice, and it is possible to pinpoint the moment of that choice. It was in the heat of prurience and wine, when a girl had finished dancing, at a birthday-party in the grim fortress of Machaerus. It is ironical that a birthday should be a day of death.

The grace of God reaches infinitely far. Herod at that moment of damnation had only to play the man and slash the bonds which held him. He could have halted short of catastrophe. He did nothing, and now, face to face with Christ, his doom was patent. Christ had no words to say which he could have grasped or understood. Here is Hell, self-made, personal, chosen.

37 : Barabbas
Mark 15.1–15

Palestine was guerrilla country of the first order. The Zealots and the Knifemen were two only of many groups which sought to make the way of the occupying forces and their Jewish collaborators difficult. Treacherous criminals for the most part, preying equally upon their countrymen and foreigners, such men of blood haunted the hills which had sheltered David and have sheltered the assassins of all the ages. And yet, in lands where nationalism and racial hatred burn like a fire, such men attain the status of patriots. Observe the priests. They had betrayed Jesus on political pretexts. They persuaded the mob to yell for their political hero with cynical inconsistency. Pilate, desperate to find a way out of his dilemma, must have seen the blatant hypocrisy, but took the risk.

The terrorist Barabbas was the sorry choice of the Jewish world. Nothing is known of this man. Picture him as the bold and dashing rebel, the idol of the mob, catching the crowd's imagination with deeds of daring, the patriot posing as the people's champion. His was no meek voice, calling to self-abnegation and endurance of wrong; he was no advocate of rendering Caesar's rights to Caesar; he had no challenging presence. He had given words to men's hate and a hand to their resentments. The world is prone to choose such projections of its own vicious ambitions and base desires. The choice is fatal. Men become like the objects of their worship and regard. To revere the man of force is to become violent. To respect the man

53

of hate and blood is to corrupt the soul with the passions of the murderer. Israel made its choice, and Barabbas prepared the spirit of the nation for the two great rebellions which poured out the people's blood and left the very land a depopulated wilderness. There are moments which, in Winston Churchill's vivid phrase, are like 'sharp agate points' on which destiny turns. They chose the bandit, and rejected Christ. The sequel was woven into history. So, too, it can be with the individual life, for nations are built out of men and women. When man chooses evil in deliberate self-will, God allows him to reap the harvest of events. 'Hold to Christ,' said Professor Herbert Butterfield, 'and for the rest be totally uncommitted.' It is safe so to be, for when the right choice stands firm the rest follows.

38 : Pilate's Hands

Matthew 27. 24–31; Isaiah 1.15–18

Over these studies on the Passion of the Lord, prescribed readings have sometimes been repeated. This is by design. We are turning attention now to this character, word, or action, now to that, and we cannot read too often the story of history's most notable event. It might perhaps help if several versions were used.

Pilate scourged Jesus and showed Him to the mob, perhaps seeking in some desperate way, to stir their pity. It was of no avail. He had tried wildly to avoid decision in the case, sent Him to Herod, offered Him to the Jews, only to find the case back continually on his own hands. One course only was open to an upright man, and all the mighty drive of events thrust Pilate to the point of decision. It was his vital test. He could still have paid the price and done the right. He failed, and sinned direly.

But Pilate felt dirty. He had betrayed justice, and justice was a Roman virtue. He took water, in a symbolic action which Jews, of all peoples, would have been most likely to understand, and washed his hands before the yelling multitude. Shakespeare had the scene in mind when he made the murderer Macbeth look at his bloodstained hands in a moment of sin's self-awareness, and know that they were beyond all cleansing:

> *What hands are here? Ha! They pluck out mine eyes,*
> *Will all great Neptune's ocean wash this blood*

> *Clean from my hand? No; this my hand will rather*
> *The multitudinous seas incarnadine,*
> *Making the green one red.*

Cleansing, as Isaiah once told Israel in his immortal first chapter, must go deeper than ritual. There is a way, only one way, he said, to purge the deep-dyed crimson of wrong from the texture of the soul, and that is by bringing it to God . . . 'though your sins are like scarlet, they shall be as white as snow; though they are red like crimson, they shall become like wool.'

Pilate had tried to force others to carry out that which was his responsibility. Now, in equal error, he sought to shift the burden of his guilt on to other shoulders than his own. Those others, in their cynical wickedness, were ready enough to carry that load, but it is Heaven's accounting in such matters which avails. Such was the folly of the procurator of Judea.

Questions and themes for study and discussion on Studies 32–38

1. A crisis and what it reveals.
2. The basis of legal justice. Can justice survive the death of morality?
3. Answer Pilate's question. List his other questions.
4. Was Pilate's wife reasonable?
5. Why silence for Herod? Are there still Herods to whom Jesus has nothing to say?
6. Life's crucial moments.
7. The character implications of avoiding decisions.

THE HOLY SPIRIT

The Spirit and the Lord Jesus

39 : Holy Child, Son of God
Luke 1.26–38

We have seen that the Holy Spirit was active in a variety of ways in preparing men for the coming of the Messiah. It is not at all surprising, accordingly, to find Him at work in the process whereby the Messiah was born. The angel Gabriel spoke of the One who was to be born in terms which make it clear that He was to be the Messiah (vs. 32 f.), as well as indicating something of the nature of His work for men by telling Mary that His name was to be 'Jesus' ('Saviour'). Mary's question (34) is a little puzzling, since she was engaged and must have expected to have children after marriage. Evidently she took the angel's words to mean that she would become pregnant without further intervention, perhaps immediately.

Gabriel's answer comes with delicate reticence (35). Here is a divine action described with reverent reserve. In this it is essentially different from the heathen stories sometimes adduced as parallels. They are stories of lust, of a god mating with a woman. This is a story of a virginal conception, an event in a very different category. The action of the Holy Spirit is essential to the whole process. The Child who is to be born will be called 'holy' and 'Son of God'. But this will be, Gabriel says, because of what the Spirit does. We generally think only of the second Person of the Trinity when we think of the Incarnation, with perhaps a glance at the Father. But Gabriel makes it clear that the Spirit is not only concerned, but that He actively initiates the process. Clearly all three Persons are involved in one way or another.

The final section of today's passage encourages Mary with the thought that what had happened to Elizabeth showed what God can do. Where the Holy Spirit is at work nothing is impossible (37). And Mary goes on to accept what the Spirit would do in her (38). It is important that we be found co-operating with the Spirit in His great work in men and not stubbornly opposing. It is the way of acceptance that leads to blessing, whatever hazards lie on the way.

40 : Beginning with the Spirit
Luke 3.21, 22; 4.1–21

Clearly the baptism of Jesus by John was a very impressive and important occasion. It marked the identification of Jesus with sinful men whom He had come to save. And as He thus was set apart for the mission on which God sent Him, He received the gift of the Holy Spirit as His equipment. Luke alone tells us that the Spirit came, not at the baptism itself, but just afterwards as Jesus was praying. If the Messiah was to do His God-given work He must have the Spirit. And the Spirit was given.

But the question remained: What kind of Messiah was Jesus to be? The Spirit was concerned in the time of testing that sorted this out. Matthew and Mark tell us that it was the Spirit who brought Jesus into the wilderness, but only Luke that Jesus was 'full of the Holy Spirit' at that time. He goes on to say that Jesus was led 'in the Spirit' (not 'by' as the RSV). It is too much to say that the temptation that followed was due to the Spirit. It was due to Satan. But we can say that the Spirit was there to over-rule Satan so that the ultimate result of the temptation was good and not evil, and there was therefore a Divine purpose in it. As Jesus resisted the evil one it became clear that in His ministry He would not be concerned with making bread or with establishing a worldly empire or with working spectacular but pointless miracles.

After the temptation it was 'in the power of the Spirit' that Jesus returned to Galilee and began His ministry (4.14 f.). Again we are to discern the importance of the presence of the Spirit if a ministry is to be in accordance with the mind of God. Jesus did not go about His preaching in isolation, so to speak, but only as the Spirit was with Him.

And in the synagogue at Nazareth He made it clear that He would do His characteristic work only as the Spirit directed. He read in the synagogue service the words of Isa. 61.1 f. with a phrase from 58.6. These words express the truth that when the Spirit of the Lord comes upon the Servant of the Lord a ministry to the poor, the captives, the blind and the oppressed follows.

57

The ministry of Jesus to the outcasts was under the inspiration of the Spirit.

41 : The Ultimate Blasphemy
Luke 11.9–13; 12.8–12

God has no favourites. If one man gives every evidence of the presence of the Holy Spirit in his life and another no sign at all, then this is not because God is more than kind to the former and more than harsh to the latter. The difference is in the men themselves. For God's good gifts, while open to all, must be sought. Asking is the first step and if we do not ask we must not expect to receive. But the genuine seeker finds (11.9 f.). Jesus makes the point that when even men, who are basically evil, give good gifts to their children we must see that God, who is all goodness, will give the best, the Holy Spirit, to those who ask (11.13). This does not mean that every casual request for the Spirit will be granted. But it does mean that no genuine seeker is refused.

The availability of this gift puts a heavy responsibility on men. Not to make use of the opportunity is a serious matter. It is in this light that we should understand the second of today's passages. The blasphemy against the Holy Spirit of which Jesus speaks (12.10) and for which there is no forgiveness is not a matter of words only. No form of words can ever be so serious that there is no forgiveness. But blasphemy can be a matter of attitude and action as well as of speech—the expression of a total life-style. Matthew and Mark both tell us that Jesus uttered these words as part of His response to the accusation that He cast out devils by Beelzebul (Matt. 12.24–32; Mark 3.22–30). To call good evil is to line up with the evil one himself. It is to deny one's best insights. It is 'the lie in the soul'. This attitude is a rejection of the Spirit's leading, a turning away from God's direction of the life, and it is this that is the ultimate blasphemy. When a man sets himself against God in this way he cuts himself off from the possibility of forgiveness. No mere words can do this—but the whole attitude of the life can.

But Jesus' teaching about the Holy Spirit is not negative. It is true that to blaspheme the Spirit is the most serious of sins and thus He gives us a solemn warning. But He goes on immediately to the thought that the Spirit gives those who accept His gracious invitation all the help they need. Even when they are in the worst troubles the world can devise and stand before 'the rulers and the authorities' (12.11) they need not be anxious. The Spirit will guide them. And if His help is adequate even for such crises how much more in the ordinary affairs of everyday life!

42 : Anointed with the Holy Spirit

Acts 10.34–43

We have seen how the Holy Spirit was active in the long years of preparation that led up to the coming of the Messiah, and in our recent readings we have been reminded of the way the Spirit was present at the beginning of our Lord's ministry and at some points within it. Now we see in Peter's speech that the Spirit was active throughout. There is still the thought of the Spirit's work in preparation, for the apostle speaks of all the prophets as bearing their witness to Jesus, and specifically to the fact that forgiveness of sins would take place through His name (43). They could do this only as the Spirit inspired them. But the emphasis is rather on the anointing that enabled Jesus to do good and to heal (38). We are aware that if we are to have any success as we seek to live for God we must have the help of the Spirit, but we do not often reflect that in this, as in so much else, Jesus is our example. He was completely responsive to the leading of the Spirit and thus He accomplished His work of goodness and of healing.

Peter speaks specifically of healing 'all that were oppressed by the devil'. In part this will refer to healing of physical illness (cf. Luke 13.16). We cannot say that all illness is directly caused by the evil one, but some is. Satan's works, moreover, do not stop on the physical level. He afflicts people in many ways. In the power of the Spirit Jesus delivered them. Peter goes on to remind his hearers that this was not a painless process. It meant the death of the Son of God (39). The anointing of the Spirit is never a guarantee that life will be easy. It means simply that God's will will be done, and that is the really important thing. And as the passion and death of Jesus were followed by His triumphant resurrection, so His followers can look for the Spirit to lead them through whatever suffering and difficulties their service of God entails into the triumph God has for His own.

Questions and themes for study and discussion on Studies 39–42

1. What values for Christian faith do you see in the virgin conception of Christ?
2. What implications do you see for your own service of God in the presence of the Spirit at the opening of Jesus' ministry?
3. 'If a man fears he may have committed the unforgivable sin that in itself is evidence that he has not.' Why is this so?
4. What difference does the anointing with the Holy Spirit and with power mean to you?

CHARACTER STUDIES

43 : The First Crowd
Luke 19.35–40; 23.13–25

The chanting, shouting crowd in the street outside Pilate's place of judgement was one of the two crowds distinguishable in the story of these days. In all crowds there is an 'activist' element which determines action and gives the colour of its morality to the inert mass. At times the vicious minority stands apart and acts as a spearhead. Such was the case here. No doubt some of them were the immediate attendants of the priestly households, or the bribed clients of the Sadducees, perhaps resentful traders from the Temple court or others who found their personal advantage involved. Others were those who, like Judas perhaps, found a passionate hope for insurrection, self-assertion or revenge, disappointed by a Messiah who had shown Himself no royal figure, no leader of rebellion, but 'meek and lowly of heart'.

Wind and wave can be ruthless, and like wind and wave are those gales of emotion which sweep through crowds and change a group of human beings into a destroying force. A crowd can be carried away by the consciousness of its own power, and the individuals which compose it are led to instincts which, apart and alone, each one might have held in check.

We do well in this mass age to note the phenomenon. It is another feature in which the twentieth century resembles the first, and we have drawn attention to the phenomenon which haunts the background, especially in the Gospel of John—the sense of the crowd, the nameless multitude which the priests and the Romans feared. When the clash came in A.D. 66, and the awful years of the Great Rebellion began, it was all because of a crowd, swept by a gale of emotion, fanned to force and fury by its 'activist' element, which got out of control in Jerusalem.

We have seen demagogues use crowds thus in our own century. The priests knew such trickery. They knew that reason dies in such heat, that what the Germans call a 'group-personality' emerges, and this can be a demon which will do the will of its creators. It is all the negation of justice, ordered thought and democracy. As Tennyson put it, watching such social phenomena emerging in his disillusioned age:

> Tumble nature heel o'er head, and, yelling with the
> yelling street,
> Set the feet above the brain and swear the brain is
> in the feet.

The noisy crowd were as spurious when they shouted, 'Hosanna' as when they yelled: 'Crucify'. God speaks to individuals. How often, as the 'demonstration' moves down the street, do we catch the sound of the old evil. It is all in the Bible.

44 : Simon of Cyrene

Mark 15.21; Romans 16.13; Philippians 2.5–11

Cyrene was a long way from Jerusalem. It was a magnificent Greek city west of the Libyan desert, a trading centre mediating commerce between Egypt and the Phoenician cities of the west. There was a large Jewish minority there, strong enough to set the place in an uproar during the widespread Jewish city revolts in Trajan's principate at the beginning of the second century.

Simon, probably a well-to-do Jew of Cyrene, had travelled 1,500 arduous miles by land or sea to attend the Passover in Jerusalem. It was the ambition of every Jew of the Dispersion to sacrifice in the holy centre of his faith once in a lifetime. Caught in the crowd, and swept along with them to the place of execution, Simon was near at hand when Jesus stumbled under the heavy crossbeam of the cross, and fell.

Perhaps Simon was a sturdy man, and rough hands seized him, flung the beam across his shoulders and forced him to join the procession of death. It was shocking disaster for the pious visitor. Not only was it dire disgrace and a bitter blow to dignity, comfort, and all that which made a worthy man's pattern of life, but the whole purpose of the pilgrimage to Jerusalem was thus frustrated. Having handled the bloodstained instrument of death, Simon could no longer keep the Passover for which he had travelled so far.

But why the personal identification in Mark's Gospel? Simon was 'the father of Alexander and Rufus'. And is Rufus the Rufus of the greetings list in the letter to Rome? It is a fair guess, too, that Mark knew the Christian group in Rome. Paul had deep respect for Rufus' mother, and calls Rufus 'the chosen of the Lord'. Did Simon become a Christian, and is he 'Simon the Swarthy' (Simeon Niger) of Acts 13.1? Did carrying the cross lead Simon to Calvary in more senses than one? Did disaster to a lifelong wish bring him to Christ in a way other than that which was visible along the Via Dolorosa?

Intriguing questions, but Mark had some clear intention in identifying Simon's family, and that a Simon became a member of Mark's circle is fairly clear. . . . At any rate, here is a man of whom we could wish to know more. His story of catastrophe strangely used of God and transformed, could help many an embattled soul.

45 : The Second Crowd

Matthew 27.37–44; Psalm 22.15–18

Round the place of the crucifixion was a larger multitude. The group which yelled outside the judgement hall was there, no doubt, and some smaller groups stood out which we shall look at soon. Voices detached themselves from the general murmur which any assembled multitude makes, and Mark's account records the fragmentary remarks best.

For the rest there was a vast inertia. The mass was composed of human beings, each drawn by his own motives, fears, hates, concerns, anxieties, to the place where evil's triumph rose so high. But all alike were helpless, as the mass of men so often is. And worse, they formed a hiding-place, a stifling blanket to cover and paralyse those who should have been seen in open testimony. In the anonymous crowd there were, perhaps, ten of the Lord's own men. Somewhere Judas was wandering. Perhaps Mark was there—a youth with a bandaged hand.

And crowds like this, inert multitudes, commonly block the way to the cross, but only for the weak and the cowardly. John, bidden to take Mary home, broke through the crowd and did his last duty. If John's account is read carefully it will be seen that it contains a gap. The events which can fill that gap may be culled from the other narratives. But what does this teach us? First that John, writing at the end of his life, was determined not to set down one fact which he had not personally observed. And, secondly, note this—the story resumes, and therefore John, in pure cold heroism, with his duty to Mary done, must have returned to the cross and taken his stand once more. He battled his way to the place where he had to be.

The crowd can be pierced. Brave men find their path to Christ, in spite of the inert horde, and through them. There is a pathway to Christ's feet from any place, any moment, any sin, any failure, any condition; and commonly it lies through the crowd. The crowd could have saved Christ. They could have over-whelmed their own vicious minority. They could have frustrated the priests. They did nothing, and so allowed evil to gain its victory.

46 : Judas

Matthew 27.3–10; Acts 1.15–20

'There is a path to the feet of Christ from any sin . . .' So we said yesterday. Was there a path for Judas? Presumably there was, had the traitor been able to summon resolution to seek a pardon. But we have seen him before. He had killed little by little and piece by piece that which, in the human heart, com-mands such response.

'Satan entered into Judas . . .' says Luke 22.3. And this was because Judas opened the way. Someone has remarked that there is no handle on the *outside* of the door of the human heart; it must be opened from within. Consciously, we 'yield our bodies to be instruments of unrighteousness'. The only safeguard is to have Christ in full occupation. To preserve and cherish un-surrendered corners of the life is to endanger the whole structure. Judas had kept his greed and ambition in a place apart. He had not set out with any notion of great betrayal, but he loved money and looked for some place of power or advantage in the Kingdom. This unsurrendered sin withstood the presence, the fellowship and the teaching of the Lord. He became harder with each day's resistance. Conscience spoke with accents more and more blurred. Defences crumbled. Then, at the proper time, Satan struck. The life which he had undermined became his to use, and he used Judas to commit the most horrible sin of all time; and having used him, he cast him cynically aside to writhe in agony of remorse.

It is perhaps idle to speculate whether such a sinner could at this point find repentance. He flung his silver down, and this is the first requirement of those who would seek forgiveness. This is where the murdering king stuck fast in *Hamlet*.

> *. . . but, O! What form of prayer*
> *Can serve my turn? 'Forgive me my foul murder'?*
> *That cannot be, since I am still possessed*
> *Of those effects for which I did the murder,*
> *My crown, mine own ambition, and my queen.*
>
> . . . .
>
> *My words fly up, my thoughts remain below.*
> *Words without thoughts never to heaven go.*

Judas was one step further on than this—but it is the last step which counts, so Judas died by hanging, fell shattered from his hanging place, a thing filled with remorse, but no salutary repentance. 'Remorse,' said someone, 'not only turns God against us, but turns us against ourselves, and makes the soul like the scorpion in the fire, which stings itself to death.'

*47 : The Hierarchy

Mark 15.16–36

From the second crowd two groups detach themselves. There was the tiny, valiant band, John and the women, who stood by the cross. There was also a pompous group of priests and scribes, who had so far sacrificed their dignity as to stand with audible comments where Peter could hear them in the multitude. He remembered their base words and passed them on to Mark. They had triumphed. Here was the one who had parried their loaded words, and flung their subtle questions back at them. Here was the man they had feared for his hold on the proletariat—here, hung high, his life draining away. They could not resist the chance to feast their eyes. They form a hideous spectacle.

Here stands man caught in the bright beam of truth. Here is the last act of his rebellion, the natural end of sin. Could the vicious depths of the human heart be more horribly revealed? Granted that they 'knew not what they did', granted that they failed to see in the tormented victim of their sadism the Son of the living God, it still remains true that they committed a horrible crime; they took an upright and gentle being, whose life had been spent in doing good, swept him cynically from the path of their own base ambition, judged him in the travesty of a trial, spiked his wrists and feet, and left him to die in gasping agony in the sun. Pitiless, selfish, vicious, cruel, Roman and Jew were here without distinction. But here too was God. We wrote above of 'him', without the reverential capital letter 'H', for a man was all that their base minds saw. But He who died was God, revealing once for all the length to which love would go to show man his sin, and to redeem him. No man has plumbed the depths of meaning of that act, but let this thought suffice and sanctify the day. Had you or I been the only sinner, Christ would still have died, for He could not be less than Perfect Love.

Among the characters of the Bible are some sights of horror and evilly marred humanity. Look at these Sadducees well. Look steadily at the experts in Moses' great books. This is what man, without God, feeding the vice of his rebellious heart, can become.

*48 : The Soldiers

John 19.23–37

The duty section from the garrison at the Antonia Fort was a brutal set of men. They were no doubt resentful of the spell of duty in a tense Jerusalem, and in Palestine the Roman legionary walked in perpetual fear of the terrorist's knife. Pilate's own harsh leadership filtered down to the ranks. Apart from the centurions, who seem to have been picked men, the Palestine garrison was probably chosen for its toughness.

They hated Jews. Hence the childish but sadistic mockery in the barrack-room, and the cruel crown of thorns. One of them drove the great four-sided spikes through the wrists of the Victim, and they all sat down under the agonized figure of the Crucified, and diced for His cloak. One of them was entrusted with the task of smashing the legs of the three crucified men to prevent the fierce lifting of the body on the nailed feet so that a lungful of air could be gasped out from the strained, uplifted chest. Thus they would die more speedily of suffocation . . . Whoever held the hammer abstained when he came to Christ and found Him already dead (and Roman soldiers, be it noted, knew a dead man when they saw one). Was this a more sensitive man who for some reason hesitated to maim a corpse? Another, less humane, drove a spear into His side, and in blood and water revealed the damage to the lungs, and the traumatic pleurisy occasioned by the scourging.

One of the band in a gust of pity drove his spear into a sponge, used no doubt to wipe blood from the hands, dipped it into the jar of ration wine which stood there, and offered it to Christ. John used a rare dialect word for spear, '*hyssos*', which some early copyist, not recognizing a genuine Greek word, saw fit to change into '*hyssopos*'. A hyssop bush cannot provide the stick which they saw from deep in the crowd (Mark 15.36). It was a spear-shaft, of course, the head covered by the sponge. But observe the accuracy of the reporting—John's use of the word he heard, Mark's or Peter's mention of the uplifted stick. Such were the soldiers—a section of a harsh world's brutal life, but graced by an odd touch of pity, one man among them perhaps. Was it the centurion himself (Mark 15.39)? He it is who would appear to have been the first of all Gentiles to accept the inner truth of the death he had just witnessed.

49 : The Thieves

Mark 15.32; Luke 23.39–49

There is, of course, no contradiction between the two evangelists. Both criminals, terrorists like Barabbas from the Jericho road or other haunting-places of the Knifemen, at first, as Mark reports, soiled the last hours of their life with abuse and blasphemy. But one must have observed the Lord's demeanour, heard His words, and remembering, perhaps, old instruction in the synagogue school, actually observed the fulfilment of prophecy. And then, in eternal demonstration of mercy and of hope, he turned, in the midst of unimaginable pain, to the Saviour.

Forgiveness was immediate and complete. The broken man bleeding and gasping to death, had no opportunity at all to do anything to remedy or to compensate for a life's misdeeds. He could only cry for pardon, and pardon he received. It is a striking demonstration of Eph. 2.8 f.—'not of works . . .' William Camden, who founded a famous Chair of Ancient History in Oxford University, antiquarian and historian, who wrote largely and learnedly in Latin, is remembered by the *Oxford Dictionary of*

Quotations for one small piece of English verse of no great distinction. It is an epitaph on a man killed by a fall from his horse:

> *My friend, judge not me,*
> *Thou seest I judge not thee.*
> *Betwixt the stirrup and the ground*
> *Mercy I asked, mercy I found.*

Legend has been busy with the penitent on the cross, giving him names like Dimas and Demarchus, and building stories round him. Nothing is really known save what is briefly recorded in this story of his pardon. The authorities, inventive in every manner of evil and misrepresentation, crucified Jesus between the two convicted criminals, in order to associate His name and person with banned political movements. It was part of the significance of the cross that the situation of sin and devilry was turned by a cry of penitence and the love of God into an occasion of salvation.

William Cowper wrote two centuries ago:

> *The dying thief rejoiced to see*
> *That fountain in his day;*
> *And there may I, though vile as he,*
> *Wash all my sins away.*

50 : You and I

Luke 23.24–38; 1 John 2.18–28

There is a sense in which we are all participants in this scene. The events of Calvary have an eternal character about them. An ancient kauri log once lay in the bush behind the house where these words are written. We set out to cut it up for winter's fires, and drove a great scarf into the wood. It exposed the growth rings of centuries. We could count back to the discovery of these coasts by James Cook. But the log was cut at one point. The same record ran up the wood and down.

Calvary is such a cut in history. Man has always been the same. As the old negro 'spiritual' asks: 'Were you there when they crucified my Lord?' We were—you who read, I who write. We are 'characters of Scripture'. With whom were we standing? By the cross with John? With the cynical priests? Hidden in the silent crowd far off, identity lost, sympathies concealed, useless, ineffective? Were we with Judas, wandering distraught?

The crime of Calvary was the work of many hands. Who crucified Christ? Was it Caiaphas and the priests, eager to conserve their life of ease, profit and comfort, and to avoid all peril of a popular movement which might embarrass them with Rome? Was it Pilate, held in the web of his past administrative mistakes, determined at all costs to protect his career, and to avoid all danger of another appeal to Caesar? Was it Herod, tangled in his sin, refusing to lift a finger to save a man of Galilee, because he enjoyed Pilate's dilemma? Was it the mob, ready enough to shout applause when they thought advantage came with the King of Israel, and who shouted for His blood when they found that He called for sacrifice? Was it the soldiers, who obeyed their orders, and drove the nails through human flesh, and diced beneath the spectacle of pain? Was it the carpenter who shaped the cross for wages, knowing that the innocent wood was to be stained with the blood of a fellow man in agony? Was it the smith who shaped the special nails, because a man must eat, regardless of the use to which the product of his hands would be put? Or was it Adam and all Adam's sons, from Adam's day to now, who have sinned and tolerated sin? There lies the answer, and what shall we do?

51 : Pilate Writes

Matthew 27.37; Mark 15.26; Luke 23.38; John 19.19–22

In Matthew's Gospel it is stated that the inscription on the Cross read, 'This is Jesus the King of the Jews'. Mark reports only the last five words of this. Luke has it, 'This is the King of the Jews', and John, 'Jesus of Nazareth, the King of the Jews'. Is there not contradiction involved here? No. All four could be abbreviations of 'This is Jesus of Nazareth, the King of the Jews'. There is, however, another and very probable explanation. The inscription was in three languages. In a multi-lingual inscription the language which is most familiar to us always stands out most prominently. Matthew, the Roman employee, would be likely to read Latin, the language of many a document in his office, with greatest readiness. Luke, on the other hand, student of the medical writers and Hippocrates, if presented with a copy of the inscription, would read the Greek, and John, the Galilean Jew, the Aramaic. If Matthew's version is written in Latin uncials, Luke's in Greek, and John's in Aramaic, they are found to occupy roughly the same space. Neatness and symmetry, we may suppose, would be the object of Pilate's signwriter, and a modification of the language in the three lines would help to effect this. Mark's version, in accordance with Mark's style, is a drastic abbreviation of all the rest.

Pilate, frustrated, and beaten by the priests, and, hard man though he was, hating them for compelling him to do a deed of bitter wrong, took vengeance on his enemies by a last insult. It hit home, as John, always well-informed about what went on in the high priestly inner circle, tells us. The priests, in the passion of their hatred, were foolish enough to protest to Pilate. He snapped: 'What I have written stands.' He used, or John used in reporting him, two Greek perfect tenses. This tense always implies a present state arising from a past event. Hence the rendering above.

The three Greek words throw a last beam of light on Pilate. Short of an act of ultimate courage, ultimate nobility, he had, he considered, done his best for justice. His wife did not think so, but, as we have seen, ancient sections of the Church gave him much credit. What of it all in God's eyes? God demands full surrender, and Pilate held back from the last brave step of committal which might have saved him.

*52 : Joseph

Matthew 25.31–46; 27.57–61

Arimathea, if the site is correctly identified, lies some ten miles north-east of Lydda, in the lower foothills of the Shephelah, the spine of Palestine. The place is named once in each of the four stories of the Lord's burial, because it was from this town that the 'counsellor', or Sanhedrist, Joseph, came to beg Pilate for the body, and to bury it in his own unused tomb in the garden.

Luke describes Joseph as 'a good and righteous man' (23.50), and John, who must have known the later years of Joseph, as 'a disciple of Jesus, but secretly, for fear of the Jews' (19.38).

According to the so-called '*Gospel of Nicodemus*', one of the apocryphal books, Joseph was the leading figure in the establishment of the Christian community at Lydda. According to other legends, Philip sent twelve disciples to Britain to preach the faith, and Joseph was their leader. They were said to have founded the first church at Glastonbury. It became ultimately the famous Abbey. Here Joseph was buried and his staff, planted in the ground, became the Glastonbury Thorn. So at least said William of Malmesbury, the medieval chronicler.

All that is really known of Joseph is that which the Gospel writers tell us. He did a humane deed in the midst of a clutter of inhumanity. His action shines like a light in the darkness. Secret disciple though he may have been, the visit to Pilate was an act of open testimony, and no mean deed of courage. Perhaps, hating Caiaphas and his brood of murderers, Pilate was not sorry to cultivate a gentleman of breeding and quiet decency. Such men were not common in the corrupt hierarchy.

Being 'a good and righteous man', a man of humane feelings and concern for the right, Joseph would also have been the first to make the facts known of the empty tomb of the Easter morning had there been possible any other explanation than that which the disciples believed—that Christ had risen from the dead. It would have appeared to such a man not only criminal, but desperately perilous to suppress the facts, if a mistake, a deception, a planned removal of the body, or anything else short of the truth that Christ had risen, could account for the events which John described, the race in the dawn to the garden, the grave-clothes lying, and 'the linen cloth that had been about His head, folded by itself apart . . .'

*53 : Nicodemus

Matthew 21.28–32; John 19.38–42

Legends also gathered round Nicodemus' name. In the apocryphal book *The Acts of Pilate*, Nicodemus appears as the instigator of a search for the body of Jesus, in keeping with Elisha's demand for such a search following the disappearance of Elijah. No body was found but the searchers did discover Joseph of Arimathea, who, having been imprisoned by the Sanhedrin, had been released by the risen Lord Himself.

Likely though the story of such a search is, at the instance of both friends and foes, the document is quite worthless save as romance, and is dated as late as the fourth century. As unreliable historically is the story that Nicodemus was alive at the fall of Jerusalem to the besieging Romans in A.D. 70.

All we really know of Nicodemus is that he was eminent as a teacher ('*the* teacher of the Jews'—John 3.10), that he warily showed sympathy with Jesus in a meeting of the Sanhedrin, on formal rather than theological grounds (7.50–52), and that, still warily, he joined Joseph in approaching Pilate with a request that the dead Christ should receive proper burial.

The courage, as well as the significance, of this act should not be underestimated. All men do not come to Christ in a burst of sudden glory. Some come thoughtfully, less emotionally, more timidly and tentatively than others. Nicodemus may have been one of those who took the longer, slower path. The general opinion is that the visit to Pilate was an act of committal, of open testimony. David Smith, writing in Hastings' *Dictionary of the Bible*, says: 'After the crucifixion, ashamed of his cowardice, he at last avowed himself . . .' Henry Vaughan, who wrote fine religious verse three centuries ago, has two puzzling lines which carry a similar opinion:

> *Wise Nicodemus saw such light*
> *As made him know his God by night.*

And with the act of mercy and final tribute, the gentle Pharisee passes from the page of Scripture and our knowledge.

Questions and themes for study and discussion on Studies 43–53

1. 'The crowd' and its mentality today.
2. 'Disaster is not always what it seems.'
3. 'Lost in the crowd.'
4. 'There is always a path to Christ.' Is this true?
5. The central significance of the cross. How would you state it?
6. Accuracy of detail in the Gospels.
7. Deathbed repentance.
8. 'Were you there when they crucified my Lord?'

9. The gospel for the Jew, the Greek, the Roman, the modern man.
10. What is 'a good man', from the biblical standpoint?
11. Nicodemus today.

THE HOLY SPIRIT

His Coming at Pentecost

54 : The Paraclete
John 14.15–18, 25–27

On the last night before the crucifixion Jesus prophesied the
coming of the Holy Spirit. He spoke of Him as the *parakletos*,
which RSV translates as 'Counsellor'. This preserves the legal
flavour of the original, for the Greek term often has a legal
application. This leads many to suggest a rendering like 'Advocate'. What such terms do not bring out is the fact that the term
is not specific. Anyone who spoke up for the accused at his trial
was a *parakletos*, and not only the legal man who looked after
the case for the defence. No one English word is an adequate
equivalent, which is doubtless why so often we simply trans-
literate with Paraclete. And some of this Paraclete's functions
are not legal at all. Thus He is to be with believers for ever (16)
and to teach and remind them of Jesus' teaching (26). The word
points to the Spirit as our Friend, especially our Friend at court.

In a sense He takes the place of Jesus, for He is with believers
after Jesus' departure from the earth (16 f.). In this capacity He
sees to it that Jesus' teaching is not forgotten (26). But there are
other things. He is 'the Spirit of truth' (17), an unusual expression,
but found also in the Dead Sea Scrolls and in the Jewish *Testament of Judah*. In neither place however does it have a content
like that here. Jesus speaks of the Spirit as specially interested in
truth (as is the Father, John 4.23 f., and the Son, John 14.6).
Probably the expression means that He communicates the truth.

We should also notice that the Spirit is called 'the Holy Spirit'
(26). It is important that the Spirit's characteristic designation is
not concerned with power or majesty or knowledge or the like. It
emphasizes holiness. We should not miss the implication for our
own lives. It is easy to be concerned primarily with absorbing
questions of doctrine or prophecy or 'secular Christianity' while
we sit loose to God's demand that we be His holy servants in the
world and to His provision of the Holy Spirit to enable us to be
so. First of all, and above all, the Spirit is the Holy Spirit.

55 : Convincing the World

John 15.18–16.15

The Church has given a good deal of attention to the statement that the Spirit 'proceeds from the Father' (15.26) and has concluded that, whereas the Son is 'begotten' of the Father, the Spirit 'proceeds' (both terms refer in the Creeds to the *eternal* relationship of the Persons). This, however, while sound doctrine, does not arise from this passage. The meaning rather is that the Spirit comes from the Father to continue on earth the work of the Son. He witnesses to the Son (15.26), He is sent by Him (15.26; 16.7), He will glorify Him and 'take what is' His 'and declare it' (16.14 f.). This vital presence is for the good of the Church. It has never been easy for Christians to realize that it is better for them to have the Spirit among them than the visible Jesus, but our Lord assures us that this is so (16.7).

The Spirit's work of convincing the world (16.8 ff.) is clearly important, but it is not easy to understand. It is the one work which the New Testament tells us the Spirit does in the world (elsewhere He works among believers). The RSV's 'convince' is probably better 'convict'. It means to bring home the guilt. The Spirit acts as Prosecutor and shows that the world is guilty. He also brings this home to the world itself (cf. TEV, 'he will prove to the people of the world that they are wrong about sin . . .'). Only the Spirit can convict a worldly man of his sin. Verse 9 may mean that the world has wrong ideas of sin as is shown in its unbelief, that its unbelief illustrates its sin, or that its unbelief is its sin. Perhaps all three meanings are present. The righteousness shown by Jesus' going to the Father must be the righteousness established by the cross, and it is there, too, that Satan is judged (cf. 12.31). But none of this is apparent to the natural man. It requires a work of the Holy Spirit for him to see it.

The Spirit's ongoing work guides the people of God 'into all the truth' (16.13). There are, of course, no finally authoritative writings for the Christian after the New Testament, but the Spirit continually unfolds the meaning of what Christ has said and done.

56 : Jesus and the Spirit

John 7.37–39; 20.19–23

Both these important passages connect the gift of the Spirit with
the Lord Jesus. The first assures us that the gift depends on
Jesus' death for men, His being 'glorified' (7.39). In John's
Gospel the concept of glory is linked paradoxically with lowli-
ness. True glory is seen not in outward splendour but in humble
service, and particularly in the death on the cross. There is no
Greek word corresponding to 'given'. The text says, 'it was not
yet Spirit'. The Spirit was not inactive in Old Testament times
nor in the period covered by the Gospels. But there was nothing
in either to compare with what happened on and after the day of
Pentecost. That day ushered in the era of the Spirit. Then 'it was
Spirit' as it had never been previously. Jesus is teaching that
Calvary was necessary before the Pentecostal outpouring. The
work of the Son is the necessary foundation for that of the Spirit.
Notice further that 'living water' refers to the Spirit. This enables us to interpret passages like John 4 which speak of 'living
water' but do not explain it.

There has been endless controversy about our second passage.
Whatever view we accept there are difficulties. It seems best to
understand it along the lines of Paul's words, 'there are varieties
of gifts, but the same Spirit' (1 Cor. 12.4). This is not another
account of the happenings of Acts 2 but something quite different.
Jesus here sends His followers into the world: 'As the Father has
sent me, even so I send you' (20.21). Then He equips them for
this mission. He breathed and said, 'Receive the Holy Spirit'
(20.22). There is no 'on them' in the Greek: the gift is to the
Church as such, not its individual members. This Spirit-filled
Church can proclaim the forgiveness of sins. Some take these
words to refer to a power given to an individual priest to grant
absolution. But the word 'any' is plural both times. Jesus is
referring to groups or classes, not individuals. It is also relevant
that He is speaking to disciples (20.19) not the apostles (and thus
not to the 'ministry'). The gathering is surely that mentioned in
Luke 24.33 ff. which included Cleopas and his companion.
Jesus is giving the Spirit-filled Church the power to proclaim
authoritatively the forgiveness of sins and the certainty of
judgement on those who do not seek forgiveness.

57 : The Promise and the Power

Luke 24.44–53; Acts 1.1–14

In both these passages Luke tells us of some of the things the risen Lord taught the disciples as He pointed them forward to the coming of the Holy Spirit. We notice particularly the stress on the promise and the power. In both passages Jesus reminds the disciples of God's promise (Luke 24.49; Acts 1.4). Indeed, in the first of them Jesus calls the Spirit the promise: 'behold, I send the promise of my Father upon you'. This unusual way of speaking stresses the fact that the Spirit is not a possession that men win by their own efforts or saintliness. He is given as God's free gift, in accordance with God's free promise.

Jesus further told the disciples to 'stay in the city' (Luke 24.49; Acts 1.4). He did not say why there should be this period of waiting, but made it clear that they should wait. It is often easier to engage in some vigorous activity than to wait quietly. But it is fatal to try to engage in Christian service in our own unaided strength. Whatever waiting is necessary must be accepted.

For in due course, Jesus said, God would send the power. He spoke of their being 'clothed with power' (Luke 24.49), and of their receiving power when the Holy Spirit came on them (Acts 1.8). If there is a time for waiting there is also a time for acting. When the Spirit came upon them the disciples would be busy, and busy in an effective and purposeful way. There is a pronounced contrast between the disciples before the Spirit came and after that event. Before, they hid themselves out of the way behind locked doors (John 20.19). Afterwards, they were different men. They made their mistakes, of course, but there is no record of their ever being afraid again. Their whole manner of life was changed when the power of God came upon them. There is more to the coming of the Spirit than power, but this is an important factor.

58 : The Coming of the Spirit

Acts 2.1–21, 36–42

The decisive empowering of the Christian Church by the Holy Spirit of God took place on the day of Pentecost following Jesus' ascension. As we have seen in recent studies the work of

Christ was the necessary precondition of the coming of the Spirit in His fullness. First Jesus must die and rise, and only after that would the Spirit be given to His followers. But now the time had come.

There were physical phenomena. The disciples heard something that sounded like 'the rush of a mighty wind'. This sound filled all the house. They also saw something. It looked like flames of fire which came and rested on each of them. But the really important thing was not anything outward. It was inward: 'they were all filled with the Holy Spirit' (4). The divine presence now filled their hearts and from this time on they were never without the Spirit of God within them. Day by day they had access to the infinite resources of God Himself. That meant new power for living and new direction for life.

As the Spirit came upon them they 'began to speak in other tongues, as the Spirit gave them utterance' (4). The subsequent narrative shows this to mean that people from a great variety of places could hear them in their own languages as they spoke of 'the mighty works of God' (11). It is not certain whether this means that wherever a man came from he would find one or other of the speakers who used his own language or whether God rendered the words of every speaker intelligible to every hearer. Whichever be the truth there was something fantastic happening, and the crowds were amazed. Notice that the characteristic of the gift on this day was intelligibility, whereas in the gift of 'tongues' of which Paul writes later the characteristic was unintelligibility (1 Cor. 14.2). These were evidently different gifts.

Peter went on to address the crowd. He told them that they were witnessing the fulfilment of the prophecy of Joel 2.28 ff. His address both brought home the guilt of those who crucified Jesus and brought out the purpose of God (23). When people questioned him he pointed out that they too could have the gift of the Spirit. They must first repent and be baptized for the forgiveness of their sins. But then the Spirit would be given (38).

Questions and themes for study and discussion on Studies 54-58

1. What connection do you see between peace (John 14.27) and the Holy Spirit?
2. What are the implications of the gift of the Spirit for the Church's mission?

3. What should the power of the Holy Spirit mean for your life?
4. What is the significance of Acts 2.38, 39 for the modern Church?

CHARACTER STUDIES

59 : Peter and John

John 20.1–10; 21.3–11

We have read from several angles the shocking story of the crucifixion as John, who stood nearest to the scene, told it.

Turn to the next chapter, remembering that, as John wrote it, the story contained no chapter divisions, no break in the continuity of the narrative. Still factual, still honest, still stamped with the mark of the eye-witness, it runs straight on. The story of the death of Christ cannot be classed as reporting and the story of the tomb in the garden as pious fiction. Evidence for truth or falsehood, as every cross-examining barrister knows, lurks in details. Ruthless dissection can always expose the plausible fabrication. Not that the broken men, who had followed Christ, were in any mood to fabricate. Theirs was no state of imaginative exaltation. They had no sense that He whom they had seen nailed, hung high and stabbed, was still with them; no reason in their menaced and perilous situation to dream suicidal fictions. They were hiding somewhere, in utter defeat and despair when Mary came with the incredible story that, not only was the tomb open but that the body was gone. It is not clear whether she told eleven or two, but the same convincing and authenticating point emerges, whether Peter and John were the two out of the whole broken band who responded with energy and action, or whether Mary, who knew them all well, chose precisely those two because she could count on such response—Peter the practical and John the sensitive, opposite temperaments, who seem to have found fellowship in their variety.

Follow them, running to the grave, the younger man outrunning his older friend. He bends down and peers in, too awestricken or sensitive to tread in so hallowed a spot. Peter hurries up. Uninhibited, practical, prosaic, he steps straight in, and only then, when John follows, is the cloth which had swathed the dead Christ's head observed, folded up apart. Peter and John appear, true to the same form, in another story. It is in Galilee, and faint dawn is on the water. On the beach is the dull gleam of a banked fire and a dim figure is standing. There is a hail across the water, and the disciples in their heavy fishing boat are told where to cast the net. The fish swarm to the right. 'It is the Lord,' whispers John, more perceptive than the rest. Peter, practical, energetic, girds his cloak tighter, jumps over, and splashes ashore. . . These stories, so factual in their unobtrusive detail, so true to the character of those who move through them, do not look like fiction.

60 : Mary
John 20.11–18

After the visit to Peter and John, and after their dawn run through Jerusalem and their discovery of the empty tomb in the garden, Mary had evidently made her way incredulously back to the place, perhaps to satisfy herself that she had indeed seen aright. She had seen no more of Peter and John, so had not, apparently, become aware of their confirmation of the vanishing of the body.

She stood helplessly by, and then, hoping again that she might have been somehow mistaken, she peered in once more (11). Observe the naturalness of all this detail. It was then that she saw the unearthly presence in the tomb, and heard a voice behind her asking why she wept. Amid the surge and play of these bewildering events she did not recognize the One who stood beside her, and thought it was the keeper of Joseph's garden.

Distracted, she asked what he had done with the body. Let him tell her, and she would take it away. How could she? She was a woman, and it would have been quite impossible for her to move the body of a man. But could any remark be more in keeping with the situation? And then He spoke her name, and in some accentuation of His voice, she recognized Him and threw herself at His feet.

There followed the puzzling remark of v. 17. Perhaps it was simply playful. 'Don't try to hold me. I have not yet gone.' Perhaps it had some meaning which eludes us. It is certainly curious that Matthew tells us (28.9) that they 'held Him by the feet'. No involved and ritualistic process based on Lev. 16, as some have prosaically imagined, is involved. Unless the remark was utterly simple, we do not understand what it meant. But this is itself evidence for factual reporting. No weaver of deception would inject into his story statements which create a puzzle. This is what Mary heard. This is what Mary reported. And Mary having reported thus, John set it down in his account.

*61 : 'And Peter'

Mark 16.1–15

Mark was writing his last words in haste. There is evidence that he did not finish his last chapter, and that a few verses were added by another hand. Mark's account of the empty tomb is therefore the briefest of all in the Gospel narratives, but in spite of this he does manage to import into the story one unique phrase: 'Tell His disciples and Peter', the command ran. The other evangelists do not report the last two words. They were meant indeed for the stricken Peter alone, and treasured in his grateful memory as the foretaste of the Lord's forgiveness. Peter, as we have seen, was Mark's authority, and through Mark, his son in the faith, Peter passed on the precious phrase to the world. There is also an unrecorded interview with Peter, mentioned in an oral tradition, which Paul passes to the Corinthian church. Paul's passage was written two or three years before Mark's narrative, and is, in consequence, the first published report of the resurrection (1 Cor. 15.5).

Was the promise to 'go before them into Galilee' partly fulfilled when the Risen Christ met the two unknown disciples who accompanied Him to Emmaus, as Luke records? The road ran that way; v. 12 briefly touches the incident. So hope came to the world; it is still the world's hope. If Christ rose from the dead, the last enemy is defeated, the man in faith can endure a world where death reigns. For death and evil are inseparable allies, and if death be conquered, sin also, its confederate, has lost its power. If such foes be discomfited, life is sweet, and, however dark the day and fierce the onslaught, beleaguered man can look beyond to the relief and final victory which are his in the conquering Christ.

Let us lay hold with both hands upon the fact that the Lord is risen. Dr Dale of Birmingham tells how that truth once laid hold of him. ' "Christ is alive," I said to myself, "alive"—and then I paused. "Alive? . . . living as really as I myself am?" I got up and walked about repeating, "Christ is living!". At first it seemed

82

strange . . . but at last it came upon me as a burst of sudden glory. "Yes, Christ is living!" It was to me a new discovery. I thought that all along I had believed it . . . I then said: "My people shall know it. I shall preach about it again and again until they believe it as I do now."' For months afterwards, in every sermon, the Living Christ was the great preacher's dominant theme. Paul speaks (Phil. 3.10) of 'the power of His resurrection'. He meant, surely, the remarkable strength and steady confidence in the life of those who are utterly and absolutely convinced that the Lord they serve is not dead but alive—real, all-knowing, all-powerful, and with them always. This is what transformed Peter.

*62 : Thomas

John 20.19–31

Census documents recovered among the Egyptian papyri, identified those mentioned by scars. Here is one dated A.D. 48, a document of the fourth census after the one mentioned in the Gospel of Luke:

> *To Dorion chief magistrate and to Didymus town clerk, from Thermoutharion, the daughter of Thoonis, with her guardian Apollonius the son of Sotades. The inhabitants of the house belonging to me in the South Lane are: Thermoutharion a freedwoman of the aforesaid Sotades, about 65 years of age, of medium height, with honey-coloured complexion, having a long face and a scar on the right knee* . . . (A line is missing here which describes a second woman). *I, the aforesaid Thermoutharion* (the document continues with an affidavit), *with my guardian the said Apollonius, swear by Tiberius Claudius Caesar Emperor, that I have truthfully presented the preceding return of those living with me, neither a stranger, Alexandrian, nor freedman, nor Roman, nor Egyptian, except the aforesaid. If I am swearing truly may it be well with me, if falsely the opposite.*

Such references abound in ancient documents, and, in fact, it was not a bad idea, for most people can find some mark of damage . . . Thomas was the last of the eleven to see the risen Christ, and he was no man to hazard life on a false report, mistake, hallucination or fabrication. Observe how conformably to his character Thomas acts. Remembering documents he had no doubt filled in, he said, 'Unless I put my finger into the print of the nails, and my hand into the spear wound in His side, I will not believe.' Such were Christ's identifying scars, and such demonstration Christ offered the doubter. 'My Lord,' cried the broken man, 'and my God.' Do you catch the 'ring of truth' in the breathless simplicity of that affirmation? 'Blessed,' said Christ, 'are those who have not seen and have believed.'

'Hath He marks to lead me to Him?' asks Stephen of Saba in the hymn which he built round Thomas' experience. He has, indeed, His marks, marks on all history, marks on countless transformed lives, and He still calls for Thomas' affirmation. No despite is done to reason in making it. Once it is made, life can never be the same again. Such committal involves all life, penetrates the whole person . . .

63 : Emmaus Walkers

Luke 24.13–35

The exquisitely told story of the walk to Emmaus is peculiar to Luke. Two Christians (they were not apostles) lived at Emmaus, possibly today's Kalonich, north-west of Jerusalem. They were walking home with the declining sun in their eyes, when a Stranger joined them. Here is a simple rendering of what followed, choosing a reading for the end of verse 17 found in the *Codex Sinaiticus*, the famous Great Bible of Sinai, and one other ancient text: 'He said to them: "What words are these which you are tossing back and forth as you walk along?" They stopped and looked sadly at him, and one of them named Cleopas replied: "Do you live alone in Jerusalem seeing that you do not know what happened there in the last few days?" He said to them: "What sort of things?" They said to him: "concerning Jesus of Nazareth, a man who spoke the words of God, a man of power in word and deed before the people, and how the high priests and our rulers handed him over to be condemned to death and crucified him. And we were hoping that it might have been he who was going to redeem Israel." . . .'

The words ring with the hopelessness of the disciples over the events which had closed the week. But set this broken spirit over against the jubilation of the days which followed. Only some cataclysmic event could have so transformed a shattered group of men. The Emmaus road saw no illusion. It was no deluded pair of enthusiasts who suddenly recognized His hands, and hurried back, forgetful of their weariness, over the seven miles to Jerusalem.

Only one of them is named. But this is singularly appropriate. Christ belongs to all mankind. A German painter shows the walk to Emmaus in a Rhineland setting. The three robed figures move among summer elms. A village church is in the distance. In the stained glass windows of a church in Fifty-Eighth Street, New York, the same scene is set in New England.

The Christ of the Emmaus road is the Christ of every road. He still walks the ways of earth with those who are eager for His company. Men are still dull and slow of heart to apprehend His plans. He is the guest of any home and any heart which offers welcome.

64 : Real People

1 Corinthians 15.1–19

Let us draw a few details to the fore as we look at the familiar figures we have followed through the narratives, as they face the tremendous facts of the resurrection. Facts they are, capable of scrutiny. E. M. B. Green aptly quotes Lord Darling, once Chief Justice of England. Speaking on the resurrection, the eminent judge said: 'We, as Christians, are asked to take a very great deal on trust—the teachings, for example, and the miracles of Jesus. If we had to take all on trust, I, for one, should be sceptical. The crux of the problem of whether Jesus was, or was not, what He claimed to be, must surely depend upon the truth or otherwise of the resurrection. On that greatest point we are not merely asked to have faith. In its favour as a living truth there exists such overwhelming evidence, positive and negative, factual and circumstantial, that no intelligent jury in the world could fail to bring in a verdict that the resurrection story is true.'

All is so intensely natural, and true to temperament and character! These people are real—Peter, ever active and practical and instinctively turning in a time of waiting and uncertainty to the therapy of deeds (John 21.3), drawing the net ashore—it had lain in the shallow water while they had gathered silent (John

21.12) and wondering round the Lord—the great fish flapping in the cords; John, following his friends, and counting the fish (He betrays more than once his interest in numbers) . . . Whether belief be accorded or withheld there is no alternative to accepting these stories as the writing of history.

Canon J. B. Phillips remarks in his remarkable little book, *The Ring of Truth*: 'I have read, in Greek and Latin, scores of myths, but I did not find the slightest flavour of myth here. There is no hysteria, no careful working for effect, and no attempt at collusion. One sensed again that understatement which we have been taught to think is more British than Oriental. There is an almost childlike candour and simplicity, and the total effect is tremendous.'

65 : Peter Again

John 21.1–19

The little church 'of Peter's secrecy' stands by the lake, its beach stony and bare, or deep under clear water when the snows of Hermon are melting and brimming Galilee high with their flood. This is where, according to ancient tradition, the Lord had His private talk with Peter, and where Peter and John walked with Him by the lake.

The conversation with Peter recorded by John is not as complicated as commentators have at times made it appear. Much has been made of the fact that in the Greek text of John's account two different words are used for 'love'. It is true that a general distinction can be drawn between the two verbs, but in John's Greek it is very difficult to define it sharply. The two verbs seem very interchangeable. Then again, the conversation was in Aramaic, and it is impossible to state whether John was translating a distinction clearly drawn in the original speech.

There is a much simpler explanation. Peter had denied his Lord three times. Each one of those separate occasions was etched on his memory. Each one cut a deeper furrow into the tissue of his brain. He remembered every stinging detail. He thought day and night of every facet of each shocking experience—what he could have said, what he should have said, where, how, why he should have retreated, resisted. . . . It all milled torturingly round in his memory, and drove him to desperation.

And now Christ was risen. Peter was beginning to see the truth of Christ's Kingdom in a new and more penetrating light. But had he, who had proved himself so weak under stress, any part in it? He did not know, and fear was added to sorrow. Christ spoke to him in the hearing of the rest, or so it seems, and three times recommissioned him and gave him a position of leadership and pastoral care. It was magnificent psychotherapy from the Great Physician. The three affirmations cancelled gloriously the three denials. Three times the words of grace and forgiveness cut their blessed channel in his consciousness. He could now never remember his fault without at the same time remembering his forgiveness, and a forgiveness charged with a task and fused with a commission.

66 : John

John 21.20–25; 1 John 2.18–28

Peter's curiosity about John is indication of the load that had been lifted from his own mind. It is a clear symptom of his vast relief, and the renewal of his interest in life. John was near them, and Peter asked after him and his future. He was gently rebuked. Let him carry on with the task delivered to him, and leave others to theirs.

The conversation was heard by the rest and remembered. The remark about John and the return of Christ became generally known in the Asian Church, in which John passed the years of his ministry. As is the way with men, the words became encrusted with what meanings others gave them, and the word went round among the Christians that the old 'bishop' would live until his Master came again. Christ, of course, had said no such thing, but it is the common way of men to make Him say what they would have Him say.

And John was inordinately old. The average life span in those days was much less than it is now. Few attained the psalmist's 'three score years and ten'. But here was John still living, thirty years after the Neronian persecution had decimated the church in Rome, almost thirty years after the death of Paul, surviving most of his fellow apostles by a full generation, outliving the persecution which had become severe in the eighties of the century under Domitian. He was in his nineties, a remarkable age even in these days of geriatric science. Hence an outbreak of superstition which set John to work again, and gave us the treasure of his last chapter.

He had finished his Gospel. He had had every reason to write that Gospel. He laid some dire heresies by the heel. And at the end of the section which we call ch. 20 he laid down his pen with something like relief. Then the rumour of his immortality reached his ears, and John took up his pen again to set the words which had occasioned such misunderstanding in their proper context. It was a weary task but reveals the wealth of confirmatory information in the possession of the disciples which did not reach the surface of papyrus. John finished his task a second time and ended with a whimsical touch which revealed that the aged man had not lost his quiet sense of humour (25). He had written well. He had woven words and teaching into a significant pattern. He had placed an affidavit in his closing section that he had written as he had seen. He had told no detail not personally known to him. He had rounded off the Bible.

67 : Five Hundred

Acts 1.1–3; 1 Corinthians 15.6; Matthew 28.16–20

Before we turn from the closing chapters of the Gospels and prepare to move on to the characters of the early years of the Christian Church, we must take note of a sea of heads—people waiting just off the stage of history. Writing to the Corinthians in A.D. 52, as we have seen, Paul set down against a report of their scepticism, the traditional evidence for the resurrection of Christ. He mentioned a group of five hundred people who had witnessed the Lord's living presence.

And, said Paul, something more than half of them were still alive at the time of his writing. Note how statistically probable this is. In any adult cross-section of the population, it might be supposed that about half would survive a subsequent twenty years. Paul must have known many of these people, and since he was, in all probability, the instigator of Luke's project of writing, the third evangelist must have met many of these people. Perhaps that is how he came to rescue the beautiful story of the two who walked to the village of Emmaus, and met the risen Christ on the way.

Some have surmised that the occasion of this large anonymous gathering may have been the unnamed mountain in Galilee. Matthew makes brief mention of it, and adds frankly that 'some doubted'. In a large gathering no doubt the personal contact and verification was less easy for some than others. On the other hand hallucination can hardly command so large an audience.

The five hundred were the nucleus of the Galilean church, if this guess about locality be true. They were people of Nazareth who had seen the town turn against its Townsman. They were people who had been guests at a wedding in Cana. They were fisherfolk of Capernaum. And who shall tell whether some upright centurion, some rescued tax-gatherer, some nobleman whose son had been ill, some man who had been lowered through the tiles of a stripped roof . . . whether these and such as these, folk like those next door, from the street below, from the farm yonder, from the shop, the factory, the school . . . saw the sight of all sights—The Conqueror of Death?

Questions and themes for study and discussion on Studies 59–67

1. The value of eye-witness testimony to the Gospel facts.
2. Why Mary first of all?
3. 'Christ is alive!' The implications of this great fact.
4. Why did not Thomas accept the invitation of Jesus to put his finger into the print of the nails?
5. 'The Christ of *every* road.'
6. The marks of reality in the Gospel accounts of the resurrection.
7. Peter's forgiveness.
8. The tasks of old age.
9. The five hundred.

THE HOLY SPIRIT

The Spirit and the Growing Church

68 : Filled with the Spirit

Acts 4

The gift of the Spirit on the day of Pentecost did not mean that on that one day alone the Church enjoyed the divine enablement. Throughout the Acts of the Apostles we keep reading of the work of the Spirit. To such an extent is this the case that it has been seriously suggested that a better title for that book would be 'The Acts of the Holy Spirit'. It is what the Spirit is doing that is important. He works through human instruments indeed, but it is the Holy Spirit who does the significant work, not the instruments.

We see an example of this when Peter and John were arrested for their preaching of the resurrection (2 f.). Jesus had promised that in such situations His followers would be given the help of the Holy Spirit to show them what to say (Luke 12.11 f.). And so it proved. When the authorities inquired of them. Peter was 'filled with the Holy Spirit' (8) and spoke boldly It is important to see that he did not glorify the Spirit but Jesus. And when the authorities heard and saw the apostles 'they recognized that they had been with Jesus' (13). The Spirit never draws attention to Himself. He glorifies Christ (John 16.13 f.).

The release of the apostles led to a prayer meeting of their friends. The praying group recalled Scripture that applied to the circumstances and saw in the fact further evidence of the working of the Spirit. They did not see David himself as responsible for the words, but God, for they prayed 'Sovereign Lord . . . who by the mouth of our father David, thy servant, didst say by the Holy Spirit . . .' (24 f.). The Holy Spirit inspired the words that met their need.

At the conclusion of their prayer the place where they were was shaken, which we should take as a manifestation of divine power. And they were all filled with the Holy Spirit. Once again they were equipped for the service they should render and the result was that they 'spoke the word of God with boldness' (31).

Throughout the chapter we see the Spirit of God at work, directing the people of God and enabling them to render the service they should.

69 : The Serving of Tables

Acts 6.1–10; 11.19–24

There was a little quarrelling among the early Christians as to who was getting the better of the deal in 'the daily distribution' (6.1). The dispute concerned the serving of tables (6.2), a task which the apostles did not think they should discharge themselves. But they did not regard it as of little importance on that account. It mattered, and it mattered who did it. So, for this work of serving tables, they urged the rest of the believers to choose seven men 'of good repute, full of the Spirit and of wisdom' (6.3). We should think hard about the implications of these qualifications. We are apt to think that a man needs the Spirit for any work of preaching and teaching. But we do not give the presence of the Spirit the same emphasis when it is a matter of administration, much less of waiting at tables. The apostles saw that there are many gifts of the Spirit and that a man needs some gift for any task in the church. So the men to serve at tables were to be full of the Spirit.

We must presume that this direction was carried out, though the presence of the Spirit is mentioned only in the case of Stephen (6.5). Now we notice a further point of importance. These men had been chosen for the lowly service of serving at tables and for that they needed the Spirit. But serving thus in the power of the Spirit they were able to do other things also. Presently we find Stephen doing 'great wonders and signs' (6.8). And when he disputed with opponents 'they could not withstand the wisdom and the Spirit with which he spoke' (6.10). So does the presence of the Spirit manifest itself.

In due course this Spirit-filled man was arrested and martyred, and a persecution of Christians was initiated. This caused a scattering of believers which affected the work of another Spirit-filled man, Barnabas (11.24). From the lowly beginning in serving at tables the Spirit led Stephen on to fuller service, and even after his death the work he began went on. The same Spirit filled men like Barnabas to enable them to do the work to which they were called.

70 : The Spirit and the Samaritans

Acts 8.1–24

The spread of the gospel to Samaria meant that, for the first time, people outside the Jewish community became Christians. The fact that Philip baptized them and that subsequently Peter and John were sent to them by the apostles at Jerusalem (14) is probably connected with this new situation. With centuries of Church history behind us it never occurs to us that Christianity could be anything other than a faith for men of every nation. But in those first days many must have remembered that Jesus worked almost entirely among the Jews (Matt. 15.24), that He sent the Twelve only to the lost sheep of the house of Israel and that the Samaritans were specifically excluded from the scope of the mission (Matt. 10.5 f.). Jesus' teaching was probably understood at first mostly along the lines of a reforming Judaism and some of the more conservative souls in the early Church would have been hesitant about welcoming Samaritan believers, particularly in view of the normal Jewish attitude to Samaritans. It was important that it be shown on the highest level that the entry of these Samaritans into the Church was welcome. So the two chief apostles were sent to give public testimony to this effect.

When Peter and John laid hands on the new believers they received the Holy Spirit (17). The Spirit comes on all God's people. There is no specially favoured race or specially favoured group. Samaritans as well as Jews received the Spirit and in due course Gentiles as well. There are difficulties connected with the delay in the gift until the apostles came. More usually the Spirit is associated with the very beginnings (e.g. Acts 2.38). Perhaps the delay is connected with the importance of making it clear at the highest level that the Samaritans were wanted. But Scripture does not tell us and we are left to conjecture.

The other point that we must notice is that the Spirit is God's gift. Simon thought he could buy the power to confer the Spirit (18 f.). But he was quite wrong. His request showed that he had 'neither part nor lot in this matter' (21). No man can control the Spirit, either to give or to withhold the gift. The Spirit is not constrained within ecclesiastical or sacramental channels. God gives the gift. All that is left for men is to receive it and to profit by it.

71 : The Spirit and the Gentiles

Acts 10.44–11.18

The story moves on. First the Spirit was given to the Jews, then
to the Samaritans. Now we read of His coming to the Gentiles,
people who by no stretch of the imagination could be brought
within the scope of the ancient people of God. In response to
God's command and under the leading of the Spirit (11.12)
Peter went to tell Cornelius and the people gathered in his house
the things God had told him to say (10.33). When he did so 'the
Holy Spirit fell on all who heard the word' (10.44). Peter immediately recognized this as just what had happened to Jewish
believers (10.47) and later, when he defended his action against
the criticisms of the circumcision party, he said that the Spirit
fell on these Gentiles 'just as on us at the beginning' (11.15).
That there was no difference between the gift made to the Jewish
believers at first and to the Gentiles now is given emphasis.
Pentecost had marked the gift of the Spirit to the Church at
large, Samaria had shown that this was not a narrowly particu-
laristic gift for Jews only, and now the happening in the house of
Cornelius completed the process by showing that God gave His
Spirit to Gentiles just as freely and just as fully as He did to the
Jews.

This was a revolutionary thought for first century Jews, and
it is not in the slightest surprising that some of the believers
should have taken issue with Peter. Typically they fastened on
the matter of table fellowship (11.3). Jews were very particular
about food laws, for they saw it as very easy to contract defilement by eating food contaminated by some Gentile practice.
Peter defended himself, first, by relating the vision in which God
had spoken to him about the impossibility of calling common
anything that God had pronounced clean and, secondly, by
telling how the Spirit fell on the new converts in Cornelius' house.
He saw in this the fulfilment of Jesus' prophecy, 'you shall be
baptized with the Holy Spirit' (11.16). His question, 'who was I
that I could withstand God?' (11.17) was unanswerable and it
silenced his opponents. But when they regained their speech they
praised God and recognized that it was His will that life should
be given to the Gentiles (11.18). They may have been slow to
change their ways, but their minds were not closed. They could
respond to a new initiative of the Spirit.

72 : The Spirit and the Missionaries

Acts 13.1–12

We are so familiar with the concept of missionary work that we scarcely pause to think what an unusual phenomenon it is. People have always been ready, of course, to convert others to their particular point of view. But it is not common to find men giving themselves over entirely to this sort of thing. It does not come naturally to men to go out with the gospel. Our passage makes it clear that initially they did so only because the Spirit led them into it.

First, He commanded the church at Antioch, 'Set apart for me Barnabas and Saul for the work to which I have called them' (2). What this work was to be the Spirit apparently did not say. And Luke does not record for us how the church came to hear the voice of the Spirit. All that we know is that the Christians were worshipping and fasting and that somehow the Spirit conveyed His meaning to them. And the believers obeyed. They fasted and prayed, which marked what they were doing as especially significant. Then they laid their hands on the apostles and sent them off. In a way it was the church that sent them away (3). But in another way it was the Holy Spirit (4). He willed that these men should go off on a missionary journey and they went. But this does not mean that the church played a merely passive part in the proceedings. The believers certainly worshipped and fasted and prayed, and we may fairly conclude that they also gave some hard thought to the situation. And as they left themselves open to the Spirit's leading they were led in the way in which they should go.

Luke does not say that the whole voyage was carried out in the strength and under the leadership of the Spirit but he implies that this was so. He tells us that, when the apostles were opposed by Elymas, Paul took action. But only as and because he was 'filled with the Holy Spirit' (9). We should surely conclude that this momentous venture was begun, and carried through, by men under the continuing leadership of the Spirit of God.

73 : The Spirit and the Baptism of John

Acts 18.24–19.7

Apollos was clearly an outstanding man, eloquent and learned. He had acquired some knowledge of 'the way of the Lord' before he comes before us, and this possibly refers to instruction received in his native Alexandria. We should probably take 'fervent in spirit' (18.25) to refer to his human spirit (even though in Rom. 12.11 a similar expression is understood by the RSV of the Holy Spirit). In this case there is no explicit reference to his being given the gift of the Spirit. Perhaps, as Lampe and others think, he had a special commission from the Lord and the Spirit was given to him then. In view of the following incident at Ephesus it is curious that there is no mention of Apollos being baptized in the name of Jesus. But we know so little about what the first Christians thought about baptism that we cannot be dogmatic in this area.

The people Paul found at Ephesus were called 'disciples' (19.1), which apparently means that they saw themselves as Christians, even though they had been baptized only with John's baptism. The significant thing about this incident is the first question Paul asked, 'Did you receive the Holy Spirit when you believed?' (19.2). It is not the question that would spontaneously arise from most modern Christians in a similar situation. It shows the centrality of the Spirit for Paul. If a man was a Christian then he would have the Spirit.

Paul found that they had known only John's baptism, so they were now baptized in the name of Jesus. The apostle then laid his hands on them and they received the Spirit, spoke with tongues, and prophesied (19.6). This is the third mention of this kind of laying on of hands in Acts (see 8.17; 9.17). No reason is given for this action in these cases only. That it was not a necessity is shown by the gift of the Spirit on occasions when it was not used (e.g. 10.44). But it is a suitable gesture to convey thoughts like fellowship and blessing. Sometimes, as here, those who received the Spirit spoke with tongues. There is no indication why this should take place on some occasions and not others. But the important thing is the presence of the Spirit, not our inability to explain other issues.

Questions and themes for study and discussion on Studies 68–73

1. What do we learn from Acts 4 about the resources open to the Christian and the way they should be used?
2. For what tasks in the modern Church should we seek the help of the Spirit?
3. What significance do you see in the coming of the Spirit to despised Samaritans?
4. What conclusions should we draw for our own work from the Spirit's actions in Acts 13?
5. How central is the Holy Spirit in your way of life?

CHARACTER STUDIES

74 : Friend of Luke

Acts 1.1–3; Luke 1.1–4; John 15.12–16

In Luke's Gospel Theophilus is 'most excellent', but in Acts he has no honorific title. Had a friendship ripened? Had Theophilus become a Christian? No one knows, but conjectures are many. Was Theophilus a high Roman official, perhaps connected with the forthcoming trial of Paul? (See Acts **23**.26; **24**.2; **26**.25 for the respectful mode of address.) Was Theophilus a secret name by which the Roman church knew some member of the imperial family? We know that Christianity had infiltrated such circles early in its history. Luke's formal beginning of his history suggests that he had in mind readers who knew the proprieties of contemporary literature. No one can tell. It seems quite certain that, whoever the exalted person was who became a friend of Luke, and the object of his books' dedication, he was real. Some have fancifully played with the thought that Theophilus means 'lover of God', and that Luke symbolically addressed his writings to all men anywhere who sought and worshipped God. This is hardly possible. Luke followed a universal practice of his day in addressing his book to a person.

It is the happy fate of some people to win immortality through a friend, a point we have previously remarked upon. Boswell would have been unknown but for his friend Samuel Johnson, and Atticus not even a name had not the great orator and statesman, Cicero, addressed his letters so frequently to him. And who would any of us be but for the fact that we have become the friends of Christ Jesus? Theophilus, at any rate, holds the distinction of being the only recipient of a personal dedication in the New Testament. If Luke wrote at his request he played a part indeed in the history of the Christian faith. It is a part which may well be played to prompt others to good deeds. It comes next to doing them ourselves. Luke's first dedication contains one verb which reinforces the argument that Theophilus was a real person. The rendering 'informed' of the RSV is not so accurate as 'instructed' of the AV (KJV). The word is one used by Luke and Paul of formal instruction in religion (Acts. **18**.25;

Rom. 2.18). It seems certain that Theophilus had heard the truth, and had been carefully taught the facts. He must surely have been a seeker whose blessing Luke sought.

75 : Luke the Historian

Acts 1.1–14; Luke 3.1–3

Luke, as we shall have occasion to note, was, in his own right, a notable historian. He professed to have carefully investigated the facts, to have tested the truth and to have been personally convinced by it himself. Every writer has his reasons and his motives, a point of view to urge upon his readers, vital information to set down and transmit. He is measured by the power of his persuasion, by the art with which he marshals and balances his facts, by the worth of what he has to say, and by the value of the history which he preserves and records. The writer's purpose can be multiple, and to compass successfully more ends than one in any piece of historical writing is a heavy demand upon intelligence and conviction. Such success is the mark of Luke's ability. More than one aim and purpose are clear in his work.

He sought first to give permanence to extraordinary events, and to record the birth of a movement which he was confident would change the course of history, and in which he himself was a privileged participant. His aim was that of the most exact of the great Greek historians, Thucydides of Athens. The Great War which determined the future shape of Greece, and ended the Golden Age of Athens, had broken out between Thucydides' Athens and the totalitarian state of Sparta. The young historian, for Thucydides was no more than thirty years of age, set to work, 'believing it would be a great war, and more worthy of relation than any which had preceded it. . .' Indeed it was, he believed, likely to be the greatest movement of events yet known in history. . . Luke might have had the very words in mind when he penned the prologue to the Gospel, of which the Acts of the Apostles is the necessary sequel. Paul was in prison. His friend set to work.

The Great Commission spoke of expanding areas of witness from Jerusalem, to Judea, to Samaria, and 'the uttermost parts of the earth', and Luke's book interprets the words. The Gospel had set out to record with historical exactitude all that Jesus 'began to do and to teach.' The word 'began' is significant. The first book was a beginning, the second records the next phase of the great spiritual movement, with Christ's power operative in the lives of His men. It was an exciting task to undertake.

76 : Luke at Work

Acts 1.15–26; Psalm 69

It is interesting to observe Luke's mind at work. In the book we are reading we shall see much of the physician friend of Paul, because a man lives in what he writes, and Luke's trained intellect is often visible to perceptive students. Observe his purpose. It was multiple, as was remarked in the last study. One aim which he kept before him, as the one Gentile writer in the New Testament, was the vindication of Paul, as the apostle to the wide world of men. Like a clever chess player, he can see many moves ahead. He stresses the work of Peter in the first half of his book, and of Paul in the second, showing how they interlock. From Peter's recorded sermons in the first chapters, Luke underlines the appeal to the Old Testament, of which Peter had in these days become most vividly aware. This was to be exactly the manner of Paul. . .

There was also another motive for stressing this incident. Peter, exactly true to the impetuous nature which found a need in times of stress and waiting to be up and doing something, proposed the filling of Judas' vacant place. He discovered Old Testament justification for this in Psa. 109.8. In point of fact, the only clear direction which the disciples had been given was 'not to depart from Jerusalem' (4) until the enlightenment of God should come to them with His Holy Spirit. God had His candidate for the vacant apostolate, a candidate possibly known to Peter.

The worthy Matthias had all the qualifications which Peter laid down. He was quite possibly one of the Seventy chosen by the Lord Himself. He does not appear again in Luke's story, which follows only the stream of witness which led to Paul and on through him. Tradition had it that he took the gospel to Africa and died a martyr in Ethiopia, but nothing certain is known. There are multitudes whose names are in the Book of Life who are in no other book.

Questions and themes for study and discussion on Studies 74–76

1. The usefulness of friendship. Consider Luke, Theophilus and Paul.
2. The ministry of writing. Should Christians do more of it?
3. 'God's man and God's time.' Can you illustrate further?

THE HOLY SPIRIT

The Spirit and the Christian Life

77 : The Spirit and the Law

Galatians 3.1–14

The great question which every religion must ultimately face is 'law or grace?' For Christians there can be no doubt about the answer. The cross is absolutely central; in the literal sense of the word it is 'crucial'. And that means that our salvation is all of grace. It is God's good gift, not something that we earn by our good lives, our prayers, our devotional or liturgical habits, or by anything else whatever. Our salvation was costly: Christ became 'a curse for us' (13). But it is complete. We are now redeemed from the law's curse (13).

Some of the Galatians had evidently overlooked this. There are difficulties in interpreting parts of this letter, for Paul does not explain in detail what the trouble was, and we are left to fill in some of the gaps. But there seems little doubt that the Galatians were first converted as they heard salvation by grace preached powerfully, and that afterwards some of them were persuaded that the path to fuller progress in the faith lay in keeping the law, as Judaism prescribed. Paul's response is to point out that this violates the central teaching of Christianity.

He assumes that the presence of the Spirit in the lives of believers is basic. He does not argue for it, but asks how the Galatians got it—was it 'by works of the law, or by hearing with faith' (2)? That the Spirit is God's gift and not the result of any process by which the Christian piles up merit is a fundamental proposition. If we had to earn the Spirit's presence, then the whole character of Christianity would be changed. Paul is emphasizing that God is interested, not only in forgiving our sins, but also in being with us, guiding us and strengthening us so that we may live lives of fruitful service. So He puts His Spirit within the hearts of all His people. Again there is the thought that the Spirit is not the preserve of a few outstanding souls. Paul adds the thought that God's gift is not something on which we can improve. We begin our Christian lives 'with the Spirit'. It is

101

folly to think we can go on 'with the flesh' (3). God does miracles in believers. But He does them by His Spirit in response to faith, not 'law works' (5). We cannot emphasize too strongly the importance of seeing the Spirit's presence in our hearts as God's gift. Take that away and what is left is not Christianity.

78 : The Spirit and the Flesh

Galatians 5.13–6.10

It is important that the Christian life is lived in freedom. The believer is not tied down with burdensome restrictions as he lives out the freedom that Christ bestows (John 8.34 ff.). But where there is liberty there is always the temptation to licence, the temptation to use liberty 'as an opportunity for the flesh', i.e. for the lower nature (5.13). There is always a conflict between 'the desires of the flesh' and 'the desires of the Spirit' (5.17). We should not think of 'the flesh' as no more than crude lust. It can be that, but it can also be a highly cultured self-centredness. It is anything which means concentration on the self and the self's concerns without regard to the good of others or the will of God. The dreadful list in 5.19–21 shows what this can lead to.

But when the Spirit of God comes into a man's life there is a new power which enables him to overcome self-centredness. This is not by pointing him to a list of laws (5.18). He lives in freedom. But in this freedom qualities are developed like love (which significantly heads the list), joy, peace and the rest (5.22 f.). These qualities are not provided by the Christian's trying hard. They are 'fruit', the natural result of the Spirit's indwelling.

This does not mean that the believer does nothing but sit back and wait for the Spirit's fruit to appear. There is nothing in our passage to justify spiritual laziness. The believer is commanded (this word is not too strong and must be borne in mind even in the midst of our freedom), 'walk by the Spirit' (5.16). He is to walk (i.e. his behaviour is to be controlled) by the Spirit as well as live by the Spirit (5.25). He is to sow to the Spirit (6.8)—perhaps placing the emphasis on future planning. He is to crucify the flesh (5.24) and refuse to gratify its desires (5.16). And throughout our passage Paul has scattered a number of injunctions to positive and negative deeds incumbent on the believer. There is something paradoxical about all this. But the believer finds in his experience that both sides of the paradox are true. He must wage a constant war against the flesh, for if he gives in to it the works of the flesh become manifest in his life. But when he determinedly sets himself against the flesh and looks to the Spirit for the strength he needs, the fruit of the Spirit is his. He does not earn it. It is God's gift. But he does not get it if he opts for the self-centred life.

79 : The Law of the Spirit of Life

Romans 8.1–27

In this classic discussion of life in the Spirit Paul draws an emphatic contrast between life 'according to the flesh' and life 'according to the Spirit' (4 f.). The 'flesh' will mean the lower nature and living 'according to the flesh', the self-centred life. Paul emphasizes the 'set' of the life (5) and points out that it is 'death' to set one's mind on the flesh (6). Notice that he does not say it will bring death but that it is death. To reject the Holy Spirit of God and to live one's self-centred life on the basis of private interests and concerns is death here and now. The man who chooses to 'live' in this way by that very fact cuts himself off from all that life 'in the Spirit' means. He sentences himself to a petty, meagre little existence, instead of 'the glorious liberty of the children of God' (21).

A second point emphasized here is the presence of the Spirit in the life of the believer. All Christians have the Spirit. Paul puts this both negatively (9) and positively (14). This sharply differentiates Christianity from the other religions of antiquity. They knew of spirit-inspired men, but they were few in number and regarded as specially favoured. It was something quite new when the Christians taught that every believer had the Spirit.

The third thing our passage emphasizes is the freedom that is characteristic of Christians. Those in whom the Spirit dwells have received no 'spirit of slavery' (15). Bondage is the very antithesis of the Christian way, for believers enjoy 'the spirit of sonship'. Now sonship in the heavenly family means being heirs together with Christ (17) and this means freedom (21). The creation as such does not know this kind of freedom. Creation is subject to futility (20) and for men who are part of creation, this means suffering (18). But for the Christian all this futility is transformed. The presence of the Spirit means that life has meaning. Even suffering fits into the pattern. The sufferings of Christ were meaningful and brought salvation to believers. The sufferings of believers have their meaning too and they are to be seen as no more than incidents on the way to the realization of the Christian hope.

Finally, Paul tells us that the Spirit helps us in our praying (26). Our prayers at best are tepid and feeble. But the Spirit Himself assists us and intercedes for us.

80 : The Gifts of the Spirit

1 Corinthians 12

It was accepted among the religions of the first century that from time to time a 'divine' spirit would come upon men. His presence would be shown by unusual behaviour, probably of an ecstatic type. Clearly the Corinthian Christians were influenced by this view and they thought that the more spectacular manifestations were, of necessity, evidence of the Spirit's presence among them. It is probably this that lies behind Paul's words about saying 'Jesus be cursed!' (3). Someone had, perhaps, uttered some garbled expression of the thought that Christ became a 'curse' for us (Gal. 3.13), and the Corinthians, impressed by the excitement with which the words were uttered, imagined they showed possession by the Spirit. Paul denies this and goes on to the thought that only by the Spirit can one really acknowledge Jesus as Lord. Anyone can, of course, say the words, but only the Spirit-enlightened man can mean them. It is the content of a man's words, not the excitement with which he utters them, that shows the presence of the Spirit. The Spirit witnesses to Jesus (John 15.26).

Paul proceeds to the thought that the Spirit gives a variety of good gifts to God's people. Nobody is left out, for to each the Spirit gives some gift for the common good (7). The gifts of the Spirit are to build up the church, not simply to please the recipients. Paul lists a number of such gifts (8 ff.). Some of them are rather puzzling and commentators find it difficult, for example, to put a clear distinction between 'the utterance of wisdom' and 'the utterance of knowledge' and between the 'through' which applies to the former and the 'according to' used of the latter (8).

There are problems also with regard to the gift of faith (9), for as all Christians have faith, this must be a special gift. There are problems also with healings (why the plural in the Greek?) and with others. We find problems also with the gifts listed at the end of the chapter (28 ff.) though without the mention of the Spirit. It is probably best not to try to work out what it was exactly that God gave the early Church, but rather to concentrate on using to the full the gifts that He gives His people today. In some cases they will be the same, but they may well differ. We should 'earnestly desire' the gifts that are best for our day (31).

81 : Love is the Greatest

1 Corinthians 13

The Holy Spirit is not mentioned in specific terms in this chapter. But it would be a mistake to think that He is not in mind. In chs. **12–14** Paul is engaged in a sustained argument about the 'gifts' of the Spirit. It is plain that the Corinthians were impressed by the more spectacular gifts, like speaking in tongues, and the discussion in ch. **12** shows that there had been some jealousies and hard feelings. Paul does not disparage the gifts the Corinthians prized. He recognizes that such gifts come from God and he thinks that all who have received them should use them. But he is just as clear that it is not these gifts that matter most. When he wrote to the Galatians he listed the 'fruit' of the Spirit and began with love (Gal. 5.22). So now he takes time to emphasize that the 'more excellent way' (**12**.31) is the way of love.

We should not understand the love of which he writes as a merely human achievement. John can say, 'In this is love, not that we loved God . . .' (1 John 4.10). If we start from the human end we shall never understand the distinctive Christian idea of love. It is God's love that gives us the clue. John goes on, 'but that he loved us and sent his Son to be the expiation (better, "propitiation") for our sins.' It is the divine love shown in the cross, where the sinless Jesus died for sinners, that shows us what love is. When a man sees this and responds to it a change takes place. He is transformed by the power of the Holy Spirit and begins to see men in a measure as God sees them, as people for whom Christ died. He cannot accordingly regard them as indifferent. They are the objects of God's love and now of his also.

The Spirit brings it about that the Christian comes to love the unworthy, love them for what God has done in him and them and not for their inherent qualities. 1 Cor. 13 spells out in some detail what this means in terms of daily living. The Spirit-filled man is mindful of what he can do for others rather than what he can get for himself. Love is the mainspring of his action.

82 : Speaking in 'Tongues'

1 Corinthians 14

One of the gifts of the Spirit which the Corinthians clearly prized was that of speaking in 'tongues'. This was apparently the uttering of sounds that neither the speaker nor any of his hearers understood unless they had the gift of interpretation. The characteristic was thus its unintelligibility (2). It denoted an activity of the spirit of the man, but not of his mind (14). It was more spectacular than love and the like, and it is not surprising that the volatile Corinthians valued it highly.

Paul is clear that this kind of speech really is a gift from the Spirit (2), and he refuses to forbid its use (39). But because of its unintelligibility he does not regard it as being as important as say, prophecy, an activity in which the hearers are edified. So he prefers prophecy to speaking in 'tongues' (5). His guiding principle is 'all things should be done decently and in order' (40). It is important that the church be edified and thus he strongly prefers the intelligible gifts. From the little glimpse he gives us of the church at worship (26 ff.) it is clear that there was a good deal of spontaneity. But it is clear, too, that what mattered most of all was edification.

A question of some importance is whether the gift of 'tongues' should be exercised in modern times. Those in the 'charismatic' movement hold that it should. Those outside it often hold that it should not. In favour of the former view is the fact that the New Testament nowhere says it should cease. In favour of the latter, the New Testament nowhere says it should continue, and in fact it does not seem to have continued. Quite early in the Church's history 'tongues' and some other gifts appear to have ceased. It is quite possible to hold that they were meant for the time of the Church's infancy. At the present time what is surely needed is charitable tolerance. If 'tongues' is a continuing gift and God grants it to a believer, he must use it. But he must not belittle another who does not have it. Similarly, he who has had no such experience would do well not to scorn him who claims it. Finally, it should be noted that there is no scriptural warrant for holding that the presence of any particular gift, be it 'tongues' or any other, is, in itself, evidence of the special presence of the Spirit.

83 : The Seal and the Pledge

2 Corinthians 1.21, 22; 5.1–5; Ephesians 1.11–14

When many were illiterate it was of little use to write one's name on anything to denote possession. But a seal with a characteristic pattern was another matter. The most illiterate and unlearned could recognize that. So when it was important that people in general should know whose an article was, the imprint of a seal would be put on it. The seal thus was a mark of ownership. When the Spirit is regarded as the seal (2 Cor. 1.22; Eph. 1.13) the thought is that it is the presence of the Spirit that shows that a man belongs to Christ. Without the Spirit we are not His (Rom. 8.9). It is in line with this that when Paul met some men who claimed to be disciples he immediately asked them, 'Did you receive the Holy Spirit when you believed?' (Acts 19.2). That is the decisive question.

In all three of our passages the Spirit is also called a 'guarantee' (2 Cor. 1.22; 5.5; Eph. 1.14). This picturesque word is used for the down payment in a variety of transactions. Moulton and Milligan cite a lady, selling a cow, who received 1,000 drachmas as down payment. They speak also of a mouse-catcher who received 8 drachmas (the rest presumably when he caught the mice!), and of some dancing girls in whose case it is specifically laid down that the earnest money was part of the full price. In each case the money is a first instalment. It is a guarantee that the remainder will come in due course. In modern Greek this term has come to mean an engagement ring, an excellent illustration of the force of the word. It is something now, but it looks for better things to come.

So with the Holy Spirit. The Spirit's presence is a priceless gift here and now. But, wonderful though it is, this is no more than a beginning. That God gives us the Spirit shows that He means business. And He will certainly complete what He has begun. The believer can look forward to the life to come knowing that it will be more richly blessed than this present one.

84 : The Spirit and Wisdom

Ephesians 1.15–23; 3.14–21

It is uncertain whether the word 'spirit' in 1.17 should be spelled with a small 's' as in the RSV (in which case the reference is to the man's inner life) or a capital (in which case the Holy Spirit is meant). There seems no way of deciding the point and exegetes will probably continue to differ. But in practice it does not make a great deal of difference. Paul is not speaking of a natural endowment, but of what the Holy Spirit does in believers. Even if we understand the text to mean 'the spiritual powers of wisdom and vision' (NEB), we must take this as referring to the Spirit's good gifts. True wisdom and that revelation that brings the knowledge of God come from the Holy Spirit. They are not the product of human achievement. This does not mean that every Christian is wiser than every non-Christian. But it does mean that every Christian who gives heed to the leadings of the Spirit is a much wiser man than he was before he became a Christian. So is it with vision. The Spirit-filled man has his vision constantly enlarged. And as his horizon extends so he grows in his knowledge of God.

Our second passage brings us a kindred thought, though this time it is more the idea of strength than of insight that is stressed. It is not easy to live the Christian life in a world like ours. If we are to do this we need a strength not our own. It is an important characteristic of the Christian way that it does not simply tell a man how to live and leave it at that. It equips him for living. Paul is fond of contrasting mere words with power (cf. 1 Cor. 1.17; 2.4) and, while the contrast is not explicit here, the power is real. The Spirit strengthens a believer 'with might . . . in the inner man' (3.16). The man in whom the Spirit lives is stronger by far than he ever was before he received the gift. And this leads on to the indwelling of Christ and to that 'being rooted and grounded in love' that leads ultimately to 'all the fullness of God' (3.17–19). It is only as the Spirit is within us that we have this gift.

85 : Exhilaration in the Spirit

Ephesians 5.15–21; 6.10–20

The contrast between getting 'drunk with wine' and being filled 'with the Spirit' (5.18) is noteworthy, especially in view of the staid and solemn demeanour that characterizes so much of modern Christianity. Clearly, to the early Christians the presence of the Spirit was an exhilarating affair and life in the Spirit far from sedate. On the day of Pentecost believers had been accused of being drunk (Acts 2.13, 15) and it is interesting to see Paul anticipating that believers who have God's Spirit will manifest conduct comparable to that of the inebriated.

It is not certain that 'be filled with the Spirit' is the right translation, for the construction is unusual to say the least. Abbott maintains that it is never used in the sense 'be filled with' (I.C.C.). It is rather 'be filled in', i.e. 'be filled in (your) spirit'. This would mean that the believer is to have his fullness in the higher part of his nature, not the lower. But, as this would take place only through the work of the Spirit, in the end it comes to much the same.

When he comes to the 'whole armour of God' Paul twice finds a place for what the Spirit does. He speaks of 'the sword of the Spirit' (which he explains as 'the word of God') and again of prayer 'in the Spirit' (6.17 f.). We should not overlook the fact that the sword is an attacking weapon. Much of the armour of which Paul writes is defensive and shields us from the attacks of the evil one. But when the Christian goes on the offensive he does so with the aid of the Word of God. It is this that enables him to advance. We must know our Bibles and know how to handle them if we are to see progress in the faith. With this we must take prayer in the Spirit. We usually see prayer as a human activity and, of course, in part it is. But it is the Spirit who enables us to pray effectually (cf. Rom. 8.26 f.). As we pray it is important to look for the Spirit's guidance and enabling. If we see it as a purely human activity we shall surely lack power in our prayer.

86 : All have Knowledge

1 John 2.18–27; 3.23, 24

In the first century there appear to have been some religious
systems that stressed the importance of a knowledge firmly in
the hands of a religious élite. Holding 'the key of knowledge', so
to speak, the possessors were able to let people in by giving them
the right instruction (and, of course, to keep them out if they
withheld it!). Only those so initiated could be saved. Christianity
came out in radical opposition to all such systems and John
insists on this when he says, 'you have been anointed by the
Holy One, and you all know' (2.20). The language is unusual,
but the meaning is not in doubt. The Holy One is the Being
usually called the Holy Spirit and His coming on people is the
'anointing'. When, then, the Spirit comes upon people they
have knowledge. They all have it. This does not mean that there
is no room for instruction in the Christian faith or for believers
going on from a less perfect to a more perfect understanding of
the faith. The very existence of the New Testament in itself shows
this to be wrong. Every book of the New Testament is written
to bring men knowledge, and there are many reminders of the
importance of studying the things of God. No, there is much
room for all of us to grow in knowledge of the Bible and of the
God to whom it points, and we can help one another to do so.
What John is saying is that this knowledge is open to every
Christian. In principle there is no piece of Christian knowledge
which is not open to the apprehension of the humblest believer.

This anointing, John further says, 'abides in you' (2.27). The
Spirit remains and continues to enlighten God's people. In this
respect they have no need of any teacher. One Christian may help
another, but in the last resort advance in the Christian way
depends on heeding the indwelling Spirit. There is no substitute
for the teaching He gives. It is imperative that we be constantly
alert for His voice and that we heed what we hear. It is this
constant experience of the presence of the Spirit that gives us
assurance (3.24). There is nothing outward and visible that shows
that God is in us. But that does not mean we are left in doubt
and uncertainty. Day by day we have experience of the Holy
Spirit and His leading, and it is by this that we know God is
in us.

110

Questions and themes for study and discussion on Studies 77–86

1. What do you understand by 'the glorious liberty of the children of God'?
2. What 'gifts' do you see the Spirit as giving to the Church today?
3. How far are you showing love in your daily living?
4. How can your gifts be used to edify the church?
5. What does 2 Cor. 5.1–4 tell us of the inheritance of which the Holy Spirit is our guarantee?
6. How may the believer be sure of growing in wisdom and in vision and in power?
7. How are you using 'the sword of the Spirit' for advance?
8. What has the Holy Spirit taught you today?

CHARACTER STUDIES

87 : The New Peter

Acts 2.1–36

It is the same clear mind which is seen at work in this vivid chapter. Luke is careful to show that the first sermon to be preached after the visitation of the Holy Spirit was delivered to a host of Jews and proselytes from all over the Eastern Mediterranean (5). The listening multitude would be versed in two languages only—Aramaic, the common language of the Levant, and the basic Greek, which had become the second tongue of the Mediterranean basin. Many might add Biblical Hebrew to their repertoire, and Roman Jews would know Latin. Jews, like Israelis today, might follow Arabic, but Jews, for example, from Parthia, would be no more likely to speak native Parthian than the average New Zealander would be likely to speak Maori. This is a 'character study' and no place to discuss 'the gift of tongues'. The writer of this note has expressed a tentative opinion elsewhere (*Tyndale New Testament Commentaries, Acts*, pp. 55, 56).

But observe the transformed Peter. Chrysostom said that Peter functioned as 'the mouth of the apostles' (cf. Matt. 16.16; 17.24; 18.21; 19.27; Luke 12.41; John 6.67 f.; 13.6). He was the chief of the band. In Matt. 10.2 we read in the list of the apostolate: 'The first, Simon, who is called Peter.' He similarly heads the other lists, but it is only in Acts that he seems to assume command and the post of spokesman. There is, none the less, a new facet to Peter's prominence, following the Resurrection and Pentecost. The Old Testament, dormant in his mind, had burst into life. It is part of the function of God's enlivening Spirit, to invest all knowledge and experience with new significance. The hymn is true:

> *Heaven above is softer blue,*
> *Earth around is sweeter green;*
> *Something lives in every hue*
> *Christless eyes have never seen.*

The truth of the remark extends to Scripture. Seen through a

112

transforming experience of Christ, the Bible becomes luminous, its words live and vibrate. Peter had a strong and retentive mind. Like every Jewish boy, he had memorized great tracts of the Old Testament in the synagogue school. The old words, in his new heart, were blazing and pulsing with new significance.

88 : The Converts

Acts 2.37–47

A solid core of three thousand converts (41), with daily accretions (47), from all parts of the Mediterranean world (5) formed the heart of the early Church. There are group characters in Scripture, and, in the familiar urbanized society of the first century, we are likely to meet with many such groups with common characteristics. It is possible to gain some idea of this considerable congregation of Jewish Christians.

They are from widely different backgrounds, as various indeed as those which constitute something of a social problem in modern Israel where Russian Jew, American Jew, and Yemeni Jew rub shoulders and learn to live with one another, with little more than the bond of a common language. These converts of Pentecost and its aftermath were drawn into unity by their common faith in a resurrected Christ—a singularly strong argument, be it noted, for the historic fact of the empty tomb. This was Jerusalem, not Rome or Antioch where certain essential evidence was beyond verification.

The converts had no thought that they would be separated from the ancestral faith which had drawn them from parts so diverse and remote to the mother-city of Judaism. History is full of the unexpected, and further enlightenment was to follow events. The Temple (46) was still the centre of their worship and their fellowship.

They repudiated a corrupt world (40), they listened, learned and prayed together, seeing no division between their religious and their secular activities (46). Did their zeal go too far? How is it that the experiment in communal living extended no further than Jerusalem, and, as far as the evidence goes, was soon modified or discarded? It is, of course, a fact that all real estate possessed by any Jew in Jerusalem was doomed, but the catastrophic events of the Great Rebellion were, at this time, many years away. A possible explanation might be that, in the first flush of enthusiasm, and perhaps in the mistaken view that Christ's Second Advent was imminent, the first Christians outran the will of God in their social organization. Then, perhaps, the passage of time and the growth of conviction modified the situation. It would appear to be a fact that a pocket of penury was left among the Christians of Jerusalem, which later required the monetary relief of the Church abroad. It is, none the less, an idyllic picture.

89 : The Man at the Gate

Acts 3.2–11; John 9.8–25

In those who are truly His disciples, the experience of Christ has a way of repeating itself. The situation at the Temple gate is not unfamiliar. Above stood in costly splendour a work of human art, part of Herod's lavish gift to Jewry, and near, according to some, to the place where doves and other offerings were sold to pilgrims. The gate, where the passing crowd was confined, was a natural place for the human derelict to crouch and beg for alms. The East has still such piteous sights to show.

The steward was ashamed to beg (Luke 16.3), and beggary takes some dignity from the spirit of man, be it disguised as the common 'tip', or practised in open solicitation. It was a merciless society. Pity was the gift of Christ, and if mercy and care for men survive a society's rejection of Him who gave them, that survival is fragile, a heritage which will erode. The psychologist Jung well remarked:

'At a time when a large part of mankind is beginning to discard Christianity, it is worth while to understand why it was originally accepted. It was accepted in order to escape from the brutality of antiquity. As soon as we discard it licentiousness returns, as is impressively exemplified by life in our large cities.'

The man whose sad presence marred the Beautiful Gate, sought pity, and received it as men do from God in ampler measure than their prayer had hoped. No word of his is quoted. He is shown, joyous in his new liberty and praising God, but, like the blind man of John's story, who had much to say, the lame man identified himself with those who had brought him blessing. His person was a testimony and it is patent fact that it

114

needs no words of exposition to make apparent to a watching world that something has happened to a personality.

The incident was no doubt one of those recounted to Luke as he scoured Palestine for facts during Paul's captivity in Caesarea. He tells it in a manner which John was to use in the Fourth Gospel—as a lead-in to an important utterance, in this case a sermon by Peter. Luke is always with us as we read his writing, and it is often possible to see his careful links in the narrative. The early Christians frequented the Temple (2.46). It was on their way to the Temple (3.1) that this notable event took place.

90 : Peter the Preacher

Acts 3.12–26; John 20.2–8

Peter's new stature and new dimensions of strength, become more and more obvious as the narrative proceeds. Alert to seize the opportunity, he turned to the crowd which had gathered round the three and turned it to divine use. This was no prepared sermon, but Peter spoke from the depth of conviction and it is of small use to speak from any other prompting. In speech and writing words come when the mind knows and the heart feels, and all else is likely to be 'tinkling cymbal and sounding brass'.

Peter begins and ends with Christ. To exalt Him should be the aim of every utterance. And to exalt Him for what He is—God's Son (13), the Holy One and Just (14), the Author of Life (15), of all-prevailing Name (16)... No diminished Christ, denied His deity, reft of His Messiahship, is potent to daunt evil and save the souls of men.

Peter was merciless with the sin which had rejected the Lord and done Him to death. He spoke with utter conviction of the resurrection. John was beside him, and both remembered the dawn race through the empty streets of Jerusalem as he spoke of their witnessing the historic facts of six weeks before. And here, in a broken man mended, was further evidence of a Living Lord.

But Peter has no harshness. Ruthless with sin, he pleads with the sinners. He points to the blindness and the vicious leadership, which had prompted the crime of Calvary (17)—a crime for which God was prepared, and for all its abysmal evil, not past the remedy of repentance, nor beyond the forgiveness of God. Here,

115

indeed, was part of a mighty plan, the beginnings of which, as the apostles' new enlightenment was now seeing, ran back into ancient revelation and the words of prophets.

And Peter ends where all sermons must end, with a plea for decision. He preached for a verdict. But why Luke's desire to report him so carefully? Because here was the very manner of Paul. Luke desired no division, such as Paul had known at Corinth. Peter and Paul were not men apart, with different gospels. Their message was one, based on Scripture, urgent, demanding faith and surrender.

Peter might have agreed with Richard Baxter:

> *I preached as never sure to preach again,*
> *And as a dying man to dying men.*

Is there any other mood for such a task?

91 : The Hierarchy

Acts 4.1–7; John 11.47–53

In human affairs it is often the sad fate of silent and helpless majorities to fall into the hands of vocal and dynamic minorities, who govern and manipulate them in their own interests. Such abuse of position and responsibility is not at all unknown in the institutions of religion. Entrenched groups determine policy, initiate action, and provide expression which in no way represents the wish of the mass. It was so in the citadel of Jewry. 'This crowd, who do not know the law, are accursed', they sneered cynically (John 7.49).

It is of little use blaming the supineness of the mass, saying that organizations and people get the government they deserve, or even pointing to the preoccupation of the majority with more profitable activity than politics of one sort and another. There are those, even in the Church, as Milton put it in *Lycidas*, who 'creep and intrude and climb into the fold'. . .

> *Blind mouthes! that scarce themselves know how to hold*
> *A Sheep-hook, or have learned ought else the least*
> *That to the faithfull Herdman's art belongs!*

. . . . . .

116

And when they list, their lean and flashy songs
Grate on their scrannel pipes of wretched straw,
The hungry Sheep look up and are not fed.

Here is the brood of them in full assembly and full voice. Note the subjects of the hierarchical grievance. 'They taught the people.' Their duped flock must remain docile in such false shepherds' hands. To teach the truth stirs awareness, restlessness with tyranny, discernment which heresy and dominance find awkward, and discontent with corrupt leadership.

'They preached through Jesus the resurrection from the dead.' The Sadducees, of course, like some of their successors, did not believe in the resurrection. Therefore it should not be preached. Truth did not matter, only the comfort of doctrine unchallenged. Facts needed no examination.

And yet how correct they were in matters of their own concern. Based on Jer. 21.12, they had a practice of postponing late judicial examinations until the following day. It was convenient to by-pass this law in the case of Christ, but how deep the hypocrisy of such tamperers with justice and the truth!

92 : Peter's Courage

Acts 4.8–22

Winston Churchill once declared: 'Courage is the first of human qualities, because it is the quality which guarantees all others.' That is true. To have the right words to say, to be endowed with the eloquence that can say them persuasively, both are useless in one who lacks the courage to speak.

Peter, who had once been daunted by the challenge of a servant girl, answers the most formidable concentration of civil power in the land eye to eye. 'In whose name?' they had asked. He tells them in plain and downright speech. This is a man utterly convinced by what he had seen that recent morning in a garden tomb, no less.

There is something of Christ about His servant. Note the echo of a well-remembered word (John 18.23) in v. 9, and catch the directness of the challenge in v. 10, and the resort to familiar Old Testament quotation in the very manner of the Lord in v. 11. Their priestly examiners, all perceptive and clever men, were not slow to recognize the source of this blazing courage. Here was boldness, swiftness of repartee in men without their schooling, and unity between Peter who spoke, and John, once more his fellow-witness, who stood beside him, which could have only one explanation—'They had been with Jesus' (13).

The admission is itself a witness to the impression which the Lord had made upon those who had sought to dash His challenge aside. And observe the unnamed hero. The man who had been healed and who was the indirect occasion for this uproar, stood silently beside them. Witness does not always need words. Indeed, the silent figure of the one-time beggar-man seems to have been the final clinching argument.

But even thus refuted they could not change. The Lord had said as much. They had sinned against the Holy Spirit. The natural conclusion should have been the admission of their need. That 'a notable miracle had been done' in no way prompted repentance, in no sense suggested that men whose policy had been condemned, stood in mortal danger if they pressed their charge. They merely judged it expedient to extricate themselves from an embarrassing situation. They sought to do so with scant success, and Peter and John, correctly assessing the measure of defeat and victory, made no move of compromise, gave no undertaking. Their insight equalled their courage. The Spirit of God can quicken the mind as well as warm the heart.

93 : The Church in Jerusalem

Acts 4.23–37; 1 John 2.15–19; 3.13, 14

The opening verse of this section (Acts 4.23) is worth a sermon. The world is all round the Christian. It is seductive. It tempted Demas from Paul's side when he needed friendship most (2 Tim. 4.10). It can deaden and overwhelm. It can destroy faith and discourage zeal. The test comes when we turn our back upon it. 'We know that we have passed out of death into life,' said the aged John with most penetrating simplicity, 'because we love the brethren.'

To be sure, the brethren are not a band of blameless saints. In the group to which Peter and John, in accordance with John's as yet unwritten dictum, returned with such significant alacrity,

118

were Ananias and Sapphira, so soon to fall into crass hypocrisy. They were none the less 'their own company' (23, AV [KJV]). The Christian should mark the onset of decay when he finds that he prefers the company, the fellowship, the functions of the world outside to the fellowship of Christians. Samson and the Philistines is Old Testament illustration.

The Church was already learning to sing: a liturgical form is apparent in these verses. This primitive hymn was built round the second Psalm. Much Christian truth was passed on and retained at this time in the form of song. It is, in fact, becoming clear as evidence multiplies, that the written records of the Church are older than was once thought. For many years now, critics with a vested interest in late-dating the Gospels, have repeatedly experienced what the late J. F. Dulles called 'an agonizing reappraisement'. At the same time, there must have been an oral tradition. More than once, explicitly or implicitly, Paul says: 'I received of the Lord that which I delivered to you' (1 Cor. 15.3).

There is, however, no better way of learning and transmitting truth than by way of song, a truth which oppressed minorities through the ages, and 'protest movements' have known. The Church, gathered perhaps in Mary's house, the place of 'the Upper Room', was aware of the fact. Perhaps the song was chanted by a leader such as James, with the group chiming in with the appropriate 'Amen'.

They were 'of one heart and soul' (32), a situation soon to pass and be riven by falsehood. The experiment in communal living is again mentioned, but observe Luke's purpose—the next story relates to sin arising from the situation, and also Barnabas appears. It is Luke's common fashion to introduce a major figure at some point before his chief appearance.

Questions and themes for study and discussion on Studies 87–93

1. The place and importance of the Old Testament (a) in the New Testament; (b) today.

2. Where and how does the New Testament refer to Christian giving?

3. Could law and order, mercy and gentleness, survive the death of Christianity?

4. What did Peter's preaching emphasize?

119

5. Are there still those who 'creep, intrude and climb into the fold'?
6. The sources of courage.
7. The place and purpose of hymns. What should hymns contain?

THE HOLY SPIRIT

The Spirit and the Holy Scriptures

94 : God has Spoken

2 Samuel 23.1–7; Mark 12.35–37

One of the great thoughts of the Old Testament is that God has
spoken to men. Expressions abound like 'Thus says the Lord . . .',
or 'The word of the Lord came to . . .' It has been calculated
that such turns of speech occur more than 3,000 times. Often
they introduce quite long sections. So here David says, 'The
Spirit of the Lord speaks by me' (2 Sam. 23.2). The Spirit is
using David as His means of communication. That is to say,
David's words are more than a merely human utterance. This
does not mean that they are not a human utterance. They are.
Every passage in scripture bears the hallmarks of its human
authorship. David does not write like Jeremiah, Paul like John.
Each writer uses his own method and style. Each employs his
own range of knowledge and skills. Each says what seems to be
indicated by the situation in which he finds himself. The indi-
viduality of the inspired writers is plain and important.

But that is not the whole story. David insists on two things:
God spoke to him and God spoke through him. This does not
necessarily mean that David was the recipient of a sudden
celestial communication. It means that God made use of David's
whole personality to convey His message to men. God was with
David in all his formative years and in all the years of his public
life. He was with His servant in all the experiences grave and gay
that went to make him the man he was. He was with him when
he came to write his last words. What David wrote was in one
sense the natural response of the man, being what he was, to the
situation in which he found himself. In another sense it was the
word of God, the word that God wanted written at that time.
This is emphasized by the fourfold repetition in 2 Sam. 23.2 f.
What David was writing was God's word.

And that is what Jesus said about it, too. He maintained that
David was 'inspired by the Holy Spirit' (Mark 12.36) when he
wrote Psa. 110. The Greek might be rendered 'David said in the

Holy Spirit' which comes to much the same. Either way Jesus is saying that the Spirit worked in God's servant in such a way that what was written was what God wanted written.

95 : 'God-breathed'

2 Timothy 3.10–17

Timothy came from a believing family (2 Tim. 1.5) and he had had the benefit of a godly upbringing. This meant that he had received a thorough grounding in 'the sacred writings' (15), i.e. the scriptures of the Old Testament. Notice that these 'are able to instruct you for salvation through faith in Christ Jesus' (15). The way of salvation may be clearer in the New Testament than in the Old, but we must never forget that the Old is sacred scripture too, and that it points to Christ.

Paul goes on to say, 'All scripture is inspired by God' (16). His word is *theopneustos*, found only here in the New Testament and not very often outside it. B. B. Warfield conducted a monumental examination of this word as a result of which he showed that it must be understood in the sense 'breathed of God'. That is to say its use marks scripture as the utterance of God. It is not that the Scriptures were produced and that then God somehow breathed into (in-spired) them. They were produced by God's breathing them, i.e. speaking them. Nothing could be said surely that affirms more strongly the reliability of scripture. God spoke the words of scripture. He spoke them, certainly, through the prophets and others, but He spoke them. It is this that causes Paul to accord such a high place to scripture.

Some translations have renderings like, 'Every scripture inspired of God is also profitable . . .' (RV). This has led to the view that some scripture is inspired and some is not, which opens the way for the rejection of what we find unpalatable. But against this, in the first place the AV (KJV), ARV and RSV translate correctly, and in the second, it does not matter greatly if we do accept the RV, for it is impossible to hold that Paul is differentiating between inspired and uninspired scripture. Nothing in any of his writings leads us to think that such a distinction was possible for him. He saw the whole of scripture as God's utterance and, however we translate, that is what he is saying here.

96 : Scripture's Origin

2 Peter 1.16–2.3; 1 John 4.1–6

The whole of our first passage stresses the reliability of Scripture in contrast to the 'cleverly devised myths' (2 Pet. 1.16) of 'false prophets' and 'false teachers' (2.1). In every century some have preferred their own ideas to those revealed in the Bible. Against this Peter insists on its divine origin. 'No prophecy of scripture,' he says, 'is a matter of one's own interpretation' (1.20). But *epiluseos*, translated 'interpretation', means basically an un-loosing, an untying. The context (as well as the word's proper meaning) is against the thought of 'interpretation' and strongly favours that of 'origin'. Peter is saying that scriptural prophecy did not take its point of release from men, or perhaps was not the result of men's unravelling of problems. He is not speaking about the way the Bible should be interpreted but the way it arose. This is reinforced when he goes on to say that the originating force was not 'the impulse of man'. Rather 'men moved by the Holy Spirit spoke from God' (1.21). His word 'moved' (*phero-menoi*) means 'carried along'. Peter is not denying the human element in prophecy. But he is denying that the human element is all there is. He is saying that the Holy Spirit carried the inspired writers where they should go. Michael Green points out that the same verb is used of a ship carried along with the wind (Acts 27.15, 17) and comments: 'The prophets raised their sails, so to speak (they were obedient and receptive), and the Holy Spirit filled them and carried their craft along in the direction He wished.'

Where Peter speaks of the origin John refers to the result. It must have been a problem for members of the early Church to know who among all those claiming to give authentic teaching about God were to be believed (as it still is). John says the test is the teaching about Jesus. The Spirit of God is known when men give clear witness to the incarnation (1 John 4.2), that is to say, when they see Jesus as the Christ, God's divine Messiah, 'come in the flesh' (really human). Where the emphasis is on anything else we are in the presence of the spirit of error, not of truth (1 John 4.6). The attitude to Jesus is the touchstone.

123

97 : The Spirit and the Tabernacle

Hebrews 9.1–10; 10.11–18

Modern Christians often find little to grip them in the detailed regulations of Leviticus. They see this book as full of liturgical minutiae, completely irrelevant for people who must live in our quite different circumstances and for whom that whole way of religion is history. Not so the writer of the Epistle to the Hebrews. For him the tabernacle belonged to a bygone age indeed (though, of course, the Temple retained many of the same features). But that was not the important thing. What mattered was that the ancient tabernacle had been set up under divine direction. The Holy Spirit of God had caused writers of old time to set down regulations for its construction and use. So he speaks of the arrangements whereby in the outer 'tent' were objects like the lampstand and the table (9.2) and in the inner one, the Holy of Holies, other objects, notably the ark of the covenant and the mercy seat (9.3–5). From that he goes on to refer to the ministry of the priests and specifically to that of the high priest on the Day of Atonement. In the fact that the High Priest alone entered the Holy of Holies, and he only on that one day in the year, our author sees the Holy Spirit as teaching men. The Spirit is showing (by the limited access granted under the old covenant) that the way into the very presence of God was not yet open (9.8). The Spirit speaks through what He has caused men to record of the old way.

The Spirit speaks also through what is recorded about the new covenant. Our author is particularly interested in the forgiveness of sins, which, he sees, could not be brought about by the Levitical sacrifices (10.11). He sets Christ's sacrifice of Himself in sharp contrast to them. Its utter finality is attested by no less than the Holy Spirit Himself, for it was the Spirit who spoke through the prophet Jeremiah when he linked the forgiveness of sins with the new covenant. Thus in both the ritual of the old covenant, and in the prophecy of its supersession by the new covenant, we have evidence of God's ways given us by the Holy Spirit.

Questions and themes for study and discussion on Studies 94–97

1. Reflect on the implications of 'his word is upon my tongue' (2 Sam. 23.2).

2. What difference does it make to a modern Christian that the Old Testament is 'God-breathed'?

3. Men spoke. God spoke. We must neglect neither fact.

4. '*All* scripture is inspired by God and profitable . . .' (2 Tim. 3.16). Not just those parts we personally find stimulating.